Selected Essays on
VALUE INVESTING

JAMES MONTIER

Published for the clients of
DAVIS ADVISORS

For general information on our other products and services or for technical support, please contact our Customer Care Department within the United States at (877) 762-2974, outside the United States at (317) 572-3993 or fax (317) 572-4002.

Wiley also publishes its books in a variety of electronic formats. Some content that appears in print may not be available in electronic books. For more information about Wiley products, visit our web site at www.wiley.com.

ISBN 978-1-118-00197-4

Printed in the United States of America

10 9 8 7 6 5 4 3 2 1

Contents

Foreword

As a conservative investment firm, it may seem unusual we would choose to send our clients essays with titles like "Placebos, Booze and Glamour Stocks" or "Keep It Simple, Stupid" written by a man who has been called a financial heretic, an iconoclast and an enfant terrible. But even if James Montier's style is brash and irreverent, his message is substantial, well researched and deeply important to those who hope to succeed as investors.

In putting together this volume, we have selected nine essays that are required reading at our firm. These essays range from such essential topics as the philosophy and behavioral foundations of value investing to such opportune advice as a warning to those who would switch out of stocks and into bonds in the current environment. Throughout, Montier presents data showing that crowd psychology and poor investor behavior tend to overwhelm rational decision making and sabotage long-term returns. But he also outlines the antidotes to these destructive tendencies including discipline, conviction, rationality and a focus on valuation.

In this time of great uncertainty, we can think of no more useful a collection of insights for our clients than this timely reminder of these timeless principles.

Sincerely,

Christopher C. Davis

1

The Tao of Investing: The Ten Tenets of My Investment Creed[1]

Many times over the years I have been asked how I would approach investing. This chapter attempts to codify my beliefs (and provide some evidence for them). However, before embarking upon a journey into my investment creed, it is worthwhile asking a question that doesn't get asked often enough — What is the aim of investing? The answer to this question drives everything that follows. I feel that Sir John Templeton put it best when he said, 'For all long-term investors, there is only one objective — maximum total returns after taxes.' Nothing else matters. Then the question becomes: how should we invest to deliver this objective?

- **Tenet I: Value, value, value.** Value investing is the only safety first approach I have come across. By putting the margin of safety at the heart of the process, the value approach minimizes the risk of overpaying for the hope of growth.
- **Tenet II: Be contrarian.** Sir John Templeton observed that 'It is impossible to produce superior performance unless you do something different from the majority'.
- **Tenet III: Be patient.** Patience is integral to a value approach on many levels, from waiting for the fat pitch, to dealing with the value managers' curse of being too early.
- **Tenet IV: Be unconstrained.** While pigeon-holing and labeling are fashionable, I am far from convinced that they aid investment. Surely I should be free to exploit value opportunities wherever they may occur.
- **Tenet V: Don't forecast.** We have to find a better way of investing than relying upon our seriously flawed ability to soothsay.
- **Tenet VI: Cycles matter.** As Howard Marks puts it, we can't predict but we can prepare. An awareness of the economic, credit and sentiment cycles can help with investment.
- **Tenet VII: History matters.** The four most dangerous words in investing are 'This time is different'. A knowledge of history and context can help to avoid repeating the blunders of the past.
- **Tenet VIII: Be skeptical.** One of my heroes said 'Blind faith in anything will get you killed'. Learning to question what you are told and developing critical thinking skills are vital to long-term success and survival.

---

[1]This article appeared in *Mind Matters* on 24 February 2008. Copyright © 2008 by The Société Générale Group. All rights reserved. The material discussed was accurate at the time of publication.

- **Tenet IX: Be top-down and bottom-up.** One of the key lessons from the last year is that both top-down and bottom-up viewpoints matter. Neither has a monopoly on insight.
- **Tenet X: Treat your clients as you would treat yourself.** Surely the ultimate test of any investment is: would I be willing to make this investment with my own money?

Over the years, I have been asked many times how I would approach investment. Until today I have always shied away from answering directly. However, I feel it is time to codify my investment beliefs. This chapter represents my attempt to set out my own personal investment creed. However, before we embark upon this journey into the murky world of my beliefs, we need to frame the question. Essentially this amounts to asking: What is the aim of investing?

THE AIM OF INVESTING

This has always struck me as a question that could do with being asked a great deal more often than it actually is. From my perspective, Sir John Templeton put it best: 'For all long-term investors, there is only one objective — maximum total returns after taxes' Or, as Keynes put it: 'The ideal policy . . . is where it is earning a respectable rate of interest on its funds, while securing at the same time that its risk of really serious depreciation in capital value is at a minimum.'

These definitions pretty much say it all. Of course, in today's world of fund supermarkets and the dominance of the relative performance derby, such simple concepts as total real return don't often feature in investment mandates (apart from hedge funds, of course). But surely, ultimately this is what any fund should strive to achieve.

Viewing the world in these terms also prevents us from falling into the modern finance obsession of alpha and beta. I reject CAPM on both empirical and theoretical grounds. Once CAPM is thrown out then concepts such as alpha and beta become meaningless, and one can focus on return generation in its own right rather than the distraction of decomposition.

Having set out our investment objective, it is time to turn to the philosophy of how this might be achieved. Below you will find my ten tenets of investment. These represent my beliefs (and in some cases some evidence) on the way in which an investment operation should be run.

TENET I: VALUE, VALUE, VALUE

At the very heart of the approach I follow is the belief that the price I pay for an investment determines the likely return. No asset is so good as to be immune from the possibility of overvaluation, and few assets are so bad as to be exempt from the possibility of undervaluation. Thus an asset can be an investment at one price but not at another.

The separation between value and price is key, thus this approach inherently rejects market efficiency (in which price and value are equal). As Warren Buffett said, 'Price is what you pay, value is what you get'. However, the aim is obviously not to buy at fair value, because that will simply generate an average return.

Rather, investments should be purchased with a margin of safety. Any estimate of intrinsic value will only prove to be correct via the intervention of luck. Hence, buying only when a large discount to that estimate is available offers protection against being wrong. As Ben Graham said, the margin of safety is 'available for absorbing the effect of miscalculations or worse than average luck'.

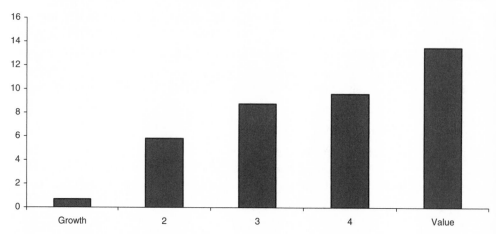

Figure 1.1   Global unconstrained value investing works! (1985–2008, % per annum)
Source: SG Global Strategy research.

Value investing is the only form of 'safety first' investing I have come across. It places risk management at the very heart of the approach. Of course, when I talk of risk management I am not talking of the modern pseudoscience so beloved by quants, but rather the 'permanent loss of capital'. Value investors implicitly try to mitigate 'value risk' (the risk of paying too much for something), and spend their time trying to figure out the degree of business and balance sheet risk they are faced with (as discussed in Chapter 2).

I would also suggest that value is an absolute concept, not a relative one. Arguing that a stock is attractive just because it is cheaper than its peers seems to be a route to disaster to me. The ratio of price to intrinsic value is the only measure that should matter.

This isn't the place for a full-scale review of the empirics that show the advantage offered by following a value approach. But to provide some limited evidence, Figures 1.1, 1.2, 1.3

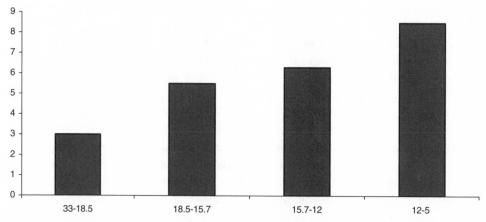

Figure 1.2   Real returns over the subsequent decade by purchase G&D P/E (% per annum) (1871–2008)
Source: SG Global Strategy research.

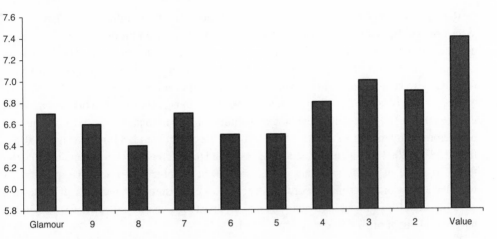

Figure 1.3 Average annualized 3-year bond returns, ranked by P/B decile (1990–2007)
Source: Brandes Institute.

show the role of value in three different contexts. Figure 1.1 shows the performance of an unconstrained global value approach to stock selection. It clearly shows the advantage a value perspective brings to an investor.

Nor, however, should asset allocators ignore value. Figure 1.2 shows the advantages of deploying capital when overall market valuations are cheap. It shows the real 10-year returns based around the purchase point defined in terms of Graham and Dodd P/Es (current price over 10-year moving average earnings). Clearly value has a role to play in asset allocation as well as in stock selection.

Fixed-income investors would also be foolish to ignore value. My friends at the Brandes Institute performed an intriguing study last year on the performance of glamour and value bonds (defined as bonds from companies with high and low price to book ratios, respectively). They find that the bonds of value companies do considerably better than the bonds of glamour companies! So yet again the power of value shines through (Figure 1.3).

TENET II: BE CONTRARIAN

As Keynes opined, 'The central principle of investment is to go contrary to the general opinion, on the grounds that if everyone agreed about its merit, the investment is inevitably too dear and therefore unattractive.' Or, as Sir John Templeton observed, 'It is impossible to produce superior performance unless you do something different from the majority.'

Following a value-oriented approach will almost certainly lead you to a contrarian stance, because you are generally buying the unloved assets and selling the market's darlings.

Rather than worry over the latest survey of opinion, I prefer to infer the consensus from asset prices. The reason for this preference is essentially misanthropy. Just as House, the eponymous anti-hero of the US TV drama, refuses to talk to patients because they lie, I am generally mistrustful of survey responses. To my mind all too often they represent where people like to be allocated, rather than actually where they are positioned.

The power of a contrarian approach has been demonstrated by the work of Dasgupta *et al.*, (2006). They show that the stocks institutional fund managers are busy buying are outperformed by the stocks they are busy selling! They examined US fund managers' filings from 1983 to 2004. Each quarter, stocks are assigned to different portfolios conditional upon the persistence of institutional net trades (that is the number of consecutive quarters for which a net buy or a net sell is recorded). A persistence measure of -5 includes all stocks that have been sold for at least five quarters, and a persistence measure of 0 shows stocks that have been bought or sold in the current period.

Figure 1.4 shows the market-adjusted future returns for each persistence portfolio on a two-year time horizon. Even a cursory glance reveals the negative relationship between returns and institutional buying and selling. Over a two-year time horizon there is a 17% return difference — the stocks that the institutions sold most outperforming the market by around 11%, and the stocks they purchased most underperforming by 6%!

Dasgupta *et al.* also noted several characteristics of the stocks that fund managers seem to buy with high persistence. Such stocks tend to be liquid, growth (low book to market) stocks with high momentum. Conversely, those that inhabit the selling portfolio are generally less liquid, value stocks with poor past returns.

One final aspect of Dasgupta *et al.'s* work is noteworthy. They estimated a measure of how likely each manager is to herd (or conform, if you prefer). They called this measure

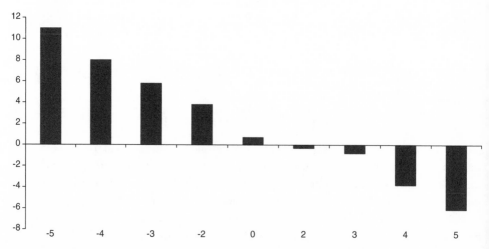

Figure 1.4   Abnormal returns over two years by buying persistence category (%)
Source: Dasgupta *et al.* (2006).

the sheep index. They concluded: 'We find that about three-quarters of institutions display conformist patterns when faced with high-persistence stocks . . . our measure of conformism is pervasive . . . with the majority of managers displaying a positive sheep value.' As Ben Graham said, it requires 'considerable will power to keep from following the crowd'.

TENET III: BE PATIENT

Patience is integral to the value approach on many levels. As Ben Graham wrote, 'Undervaluations caused by neglect or prejudice may persist for an inconveniently long time, and the same applies to inflated prices caused by over-enthusiasm or artificial stimulants.'

Whenever a position is put on, one can never be sure whether it will work or not. Buying cheap stocks helps to generate long-run returns, but tells us nothing about the short-term prospects. Cheap stocks can always get cheaper, and expensive stocks can always get more expensive (in the short term).

Thus patience is required. At the stock level, a value situation can lead to one of three possible outcomes:

1. A stock may rerate as the market corrects the underpricing.
2. The stock may stay depressed, but potentially generate a return through higher dividend payments.
3. The stock may never recover (aka value traps).

So patience is a prerequisite for value managers as long as we are dealing with the first two types of stocks, and a key problem when it comes to the third type of stock. Figure 1.5 shows the need for patience when it comes to global value investing.

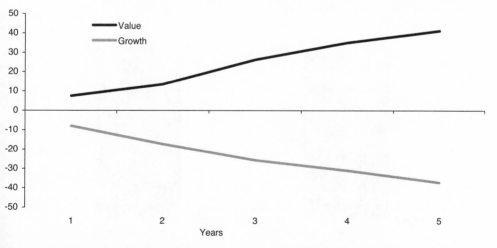

Figure 1.5   Patience is a virtue: cumulative excess returns over various holding periods
Source: SG Global Strategy research.

The value strategy tends to outperform the market by around 7% in the first year. If you hold for another 12 months, an additional 6% is added to the return. However, holding for longer periods really creates opportunity. In the third year an amazing 12% outperformance of the market is recorded, followed by another 8% in the fourth year.

This receives practical support when one examines the average holding period of long-term successful value managers; their average holding period is around five years. A marked contrast to the churn and burn of the average mutual fund (Figure 1.6).

A long time horizon makes sense from the perspective of the drivers of returns as well. For instance, on a one-year view, 60% of your total return comes through changes in valuation (effectively random fluctuations in prices about which I know nothing). However, as we extend the time horizon, so the things I, as a fundamental investor, am meant to understand start to matter much more. For instance, over a five-year horizon, some 80% of the total real return is generated through the price I pay and the growth in the underlying business.

However, it appears as if patient long-term investors are a vanishing species. As Keynes noted, 'Compared with their predecessors, modern investors concentrate too much on annual, quarterly, or even monthly valuations of what they hold, and on capital appreciation. . . . And too little on immediate yield. . . . And intrinsic worth.'

As Figure 1.7 shows, the average investor appears to have a chronic case of attention deficit hyperactivity disorder. The average holding period for a stock on the NYSE is six months! Under this time horizon, the only thing that any one cares about is: what is going to happen next quarter?

As Keynes opined, 'The spectacle of modern investment markets has sometimes moved me towards the conclusion that to make the purchase of an investment permanent and indissoluble, like marriage, except by reason of death or other grave cause, might be a useful remedy for our contemporary evils. For this would force the investor to direct his mind to the long-term prospects and to those only.'

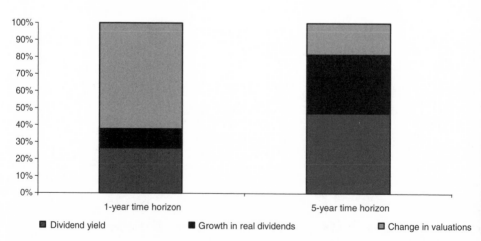

Figure 1.6 Contribution to total real return depends on your time horizon — US data since 1871
Source: SG Global Strategy research.

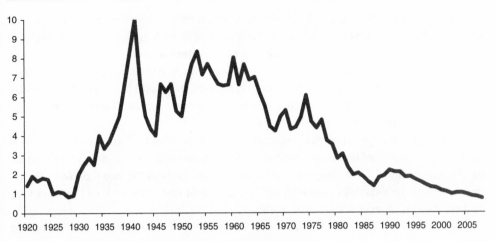

Figure 1.7   Average holding period for a stock on the NYSE (years)
Source: SG Global Strategy research.

Of course, the obsession with the short-term creates an opportunity. If everyone else is dashing around pricing assets on the basis of the next three months, then they are likely to mis-price assets for the longer term. So an opportunity for time arbitrage arises for the investor with a longer horizon. Sadly, as Keynes observed, 'investment based on genuine long-term expectation is so difficult today as to be scarcely practicable'.

This is not to say that the value approach leads one to be totally immune from the market. In the event of a value trap, patience can lead to disaster. To guard against this possibility, a lot of time should be spent on reviewing positions that move against you. If a position goes 'bad' then a review should be triggered. The aim of the review should be to start from a blank sheet of paper and consider what should be done now.

If nothing fundamental has changed (i.e. this is just a case of price volatility being an order of magnitude higher than fundamental volatility) then the opportunity arises for an increase in the position (assuming limits haven't been hit). If something fundamental and material has changed, then the position can be cut.

Accepting the integral role of patience also means that leverage will be avoided. Leverage limits the staying power of an investor and thus must be shunned. As Keynes observed, 'An investor who proposes to ignore near-term market fluctuations needs greater resources for safety and must not operate on so large a scale, if at all, with borrowed money.'

Patience is also required because the curse of the value manager is to be too early — both in terms of the buy (known affectionately as premature accumulation) and sell decisions. Unfortunately, in the short term being early is indistinguishable from being wrong.

We followers of value tend to get out of positions when they start to look expensive, rather than when they look ridiculously overvalued. My own work is a litany of premature problem spotting. For instance, calling Thailand the next Mexico in 1995, arguing that the equity market was enjoying one last hurrah in 1997 (before losing my head in the mania of the tech bubble), pointing out the bubble characteristics of both the US housing market and commodities in 2005, and calling the mining sector a bubble in 2006.

If I was clairvoyant, I would be fully invested until the day before the crash and never buy until the bottom. However, since I don't possess a crystal ball (and I haven't met anyone else who does), I can see no alternative but to continue to act in a patient, cautious fashion. This means that positions need to be built slowly over time.

Patience is also required when the bottom-up search for value fails to uncover anything of merit. I have suggested that most investors suffer an action bias — effectively a propensity to 'do' something. I have long found succour in the words of Winnie-the-Pooh, 'Never underestimate the value of doing nothing.' If I can't find something to invest in, then I am best off doing nothing at all.

Warren Buffett often talks of the importance of waiting for the 'fat pitch'. 'I call investing the greatest business in the world,' he says, 'because you never have to swing. You stand at the plate, the pitcher throws you General Motors at 47! U.S. Steel at 39! and nobody calls a strike on you. There's no penalty except opportunity lost. All day you wait for the pitch you like; then when the fielders are asleep, you step up and hit it.'

However, most institutional investors behave 'like Babe Ruth at bat with 50,000 fans and the club owner yelling, "Swing, you bum!" and some guy is trying to intentionally walk him. They know if they don't take a swing at the next pitch, the guy will say, "Turn in your uniform".'

Buffett often refers to *The Science of Hitting*, a book written by Red Sox legend Ted Williams. In it, Williams describes part of the secret to his phenomenal .344 career batting average. The theory behind Williams' extraordinary success was really quite simple (as many of the best ideas generally are).

He split the strike zone into 77 cells, each of which made up the size of a baseball, and rather than swing at anything that made its way into the strike zone, he would swing only at balls within his best cells, the sweet spot — the ones he knew he could hit. If balls didn't enter his best cell, he simply waited for the next one — even if it meant striking out now and then.

Thus, just as Williams wouldn't swing at everything, investors should wait for the fat pitch. Thus when the bottom-up search for opportunities fails, investors would be well advised to hold cash. As the Sage of Omaha has said, 'Holding cash is uncomfortable, but not as uncomfortable as doing something stupid.'

TENET IV: BE UNCONSTRAINED

One of the evils of modern-day finance is an obsession with pigeon-holing managers. This has always struck me as slightly daft. If I have a good manager, why wouldn't I want him to invest where he thought the opportunity lay?

For instance, in my work I have been trying to construct a portfolio of assets based around three themes: cash as a hedge against deflation (and to act as a feeder to deploy capital into my other two categories), deep value opportunities in both fixed income and equity space and, finally, sources of cheap insurance such as TIPS, gold and dividend swaps.

Of course today, most managers are forced to be specialist, leaving the 'asset allocation' decisions to the end client (a group who generally have an even more tenuous grasp on how to invest than the average fund managers). These constraints prevent investors from exploiting the full range of the opportunity set they are confronted by. A portfolio such as the one I have outlined would be unthinkable to many investors, or would require a large number of specialist managers.

Similarly, there may be times, like last year, when my analysis tells me the best place to be is net short. Early last year, my screens were throwing up the highest number of short ideas I have ever seen. Simultaneously, the long side was pretty much bereft of potential opportunities. This was a clear signal that the advantage was on the short side. Yet many managers found themselves constrained to be fully invested!

Artificially constraining a manager seems to be like hiring Robert Plant but telling him he can only sing lullabies. As long as I find investments within my 'circle of competence', to borrow Buffett's phraseology, why shouldn't I be free to exploit them?

TENET V: DON'T FORECAST

I have tried to make this a list of do's rather than a list of don'ts but I have to include one giant DON'T. The folly of forecasting is one of my pet hobby-horses. I simply can't understand why so many investors spend so much time engaged in an activity that has so little value, and so little chance of success.

For instance, let's say you invest according to the following process: forecast the economy, forecast the path of interest rates, forecast the sectors that will do well within that environment, and finally forecast the stocks that will do well within that sector.

Now let's assume you are pretty good at this and you are right on each forecast 70% of the time (massively above the rates actually seen). However, if you require all four forecasts to be correct, then you have just a 24% chance of actually getting it right! (This assumes that each of the forecasts is an independent event.) Now think about the number of forecasts an average analyst model contains. Sales, costs, taxes, etc. — no wonder these guys are never right.

In addition, even if by some miracle of divine intervention your forecast turns out to be correct, you can only make money from it, if (and only if) it is different from the consensus. This adds a whole new dimension of complexity to the problem.

Organizations like Starmine take great pride in revealing who the most accurate analyst is each year. However, if you cast your eye down the list of winners, sadly there is very little persistence. Effectively, this suggests that a 'lucky fool' won the competition with an outlier forecast. It should also be noted that each year someone has to be the most accurate analyst! It doesn't mean they were actually right, potentially they were just less wrong than their brethren.

The evidence on the folly of forecasting is overwhelming and would fill many notes in its own right. However, let's just skate through a few charts which show just how appalling forecasting really is. Let's start at the top, the economists. These guys haven't got a clue. Frankly, the three blind mice have more credibility than any macro-forecaster at seeing what is coming. Figure 1.8 shows that they constantly fail to predict recessions (until we are firmly in one), and even then they do so only under duress.

The analysts are no better. Their forecasting record is simply dreadful on both short- and long-term issues. My colleague Rui Antunes has examined the accuracy of analysts. Rather than doing the analysis at the aggregate level (as I have done in the past) Rui, ever the pedant, has investigated the scale of the error at the individual stock level.

Figure 1.9 shows the average scale of the analysts' forecast errors over time. In the US, the average 24-month forecast error is 93%, and the average 12-month forecast error is 47% over the period 2001–2006. The data for Europe is no less disconcerting. The average 24-month forecast error is 95%, and the average 12-month forecast error is 43%. To put it mildly, analysts don't have a clue about future earnings.

Analysts' performance in divining the longer-term future is sadly no better than their performance in the short term. Figure 1.10 shows the five-year forward growth rates from analysts, and the actual outturns. Quintile 5 are all the stocks the analysts expect to grow fast, and quintile 1 are the stocks the analysts expect to grow slowly.

Even a cursory glance at the chart reveals that the outcomes show no statistical difference across quintiles. That is to say, analysts have absolutely no idea about forecasting long-term growth.

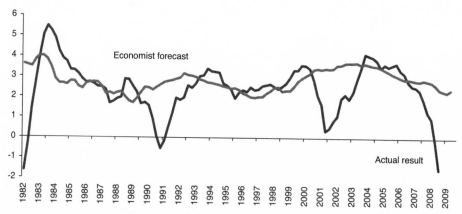

Figure 1.8   US GDP and economists' forecasts (4q ma, %)
Source: SG Global Strategy research.

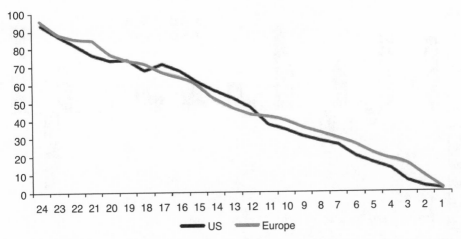

Figure 1.9 Forecast error over time: US and European markets 2001–2006, %
Source: SG Global Strategy research.

My final rant on the folly of forecasting concerns target prices. Why do analysts persist in trying to forecast prices? As Ben Graham said, 'Forecasting security prices is not properly a part of security analysis.'

Figure 1.11 shows the embarrassing track record that analysts have managed to rack up with respect to target prices. For each year, I have taken the price of the security at the start of the year, and assumed that the analysts' target price is a view of where the price should be in 12 months' time. On average the analysts expect stocks to be 25% higher each year!

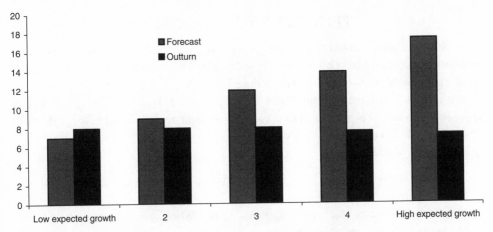

Figure 1.10 Long-term growth forecasts and outcomes (US, 1982–2008, %)
Source: SG Global Strategy research.

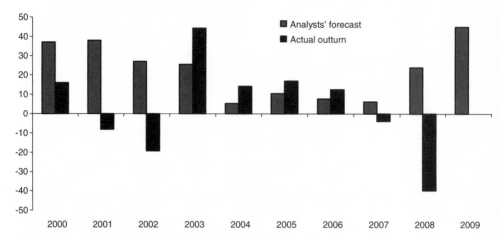

Figure 1.11 Analyst expected returns (via target prices) and actual returns (US, %)
Source: SG Global Strategy research.

I have then contrasted this implied analyst view with the actual returns achieved across the same universe. As you can see, the results are not favorable to the worth of target prices. In four out of the nine years, analysts have not even managed to get the direction of change in prices correct! The absolute scale of the average forecast error is 25%.

The bottom line from this whistle-stop tour of the failure of forecasting is that it would be sheer madness to base an investment process around our seriously flawed ability to divine the future. We would all be better off if we took Keynes suggested response when asked about the future, 'We simply do not know.'

TENET VI: CYCLES MATTER

The sixth tenet that I would like to suggest is that cycles matter — even for long-term investors. As Howard Marks of Oaktree Capital puts it, while we may not be able to predict, we can prepare. All sorts of cycles exist, economic, credit, and sentiment, to name but three.

It is often said that markets are driven by fear and greed. However, they generally only appear one at a time. The market's mood swings from irrational exuberance, to the depths of despair. Mr. Market really is a manic depressive.

As Howard Marks wrote:

'In my opinion, there are two key concepts that investors must master: value and cycles. For each asset you're considering, you must have a strongly held view of its intrinsic value. When its price is below that value, it's generally a buy. When its price is higher, it's a sell. In a nutshell, that's value investing.'

But values aren't fixed; they move in response to changes in the economic environment. Thus, cyclical considerations influence an asset's current value. Value depends on earnings, for example, and earnings are shaped by the economic cycle and the price being charged for liquidity.

Further, security prices are greatly affected by investor behavior; thus we can be aided in investing safely by understanding where we stand in terms of the market cycle. What's going on in terms of investor psychology, and how does it tell us to act in the short run? We want to buy when prices seem attractive. But if investors are giddy and optimism is rampant, we have to consider whether a better buying opportunity mightn't come along later.

One of our proxies for where we stand is shown in Figure 1.12. It attempts in a simplistic fashion to measure where we stand in the oscillations between the zenith of euphoria and the nadir of despair. I certainly can't predict where it is going, but I can prepare for the swings, and try to take advantage of the opportunity set that is created by these swings. It gives rise to a sliding scale of capital commitment driven by a desire to lean against the wind.

In part this is obviously strongly related to Tenet II on being contrarian. As Sir John Templeton said, 'To buy when others are despondently selling and to sell when others are avidly buying requires the greatest fortitude and pays the greatest rewards.'

As Seth Klarman notes in *Margin of Safety:*

There are many explanations for volatility in business value. The 'credit cycle', the periodic tightening and relaxation of the availability of credit, is a major factor, for example, because it influences the cost and terms upon which money can be borrowed. This in turn affects the multiples that buyers are willing to pay for businesses. Simply put, buyers will willingly pay higher multiples if they receive low-rate non-recourse financing than they will in an unleveraged transaction.

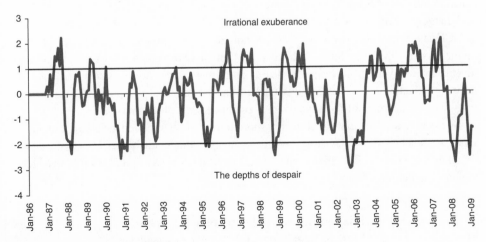

Figure 1.12 Our fear and greed index
Source: SG Global Strategy research.

Remembering that cycles occur is of vital importance, for it helps to remind one to sell as things become dear, and buy as they become cheap. But it also reinforces the need for slow position building, as we never know if we are at the top or the bottom of a cycle until after it has passed.

TENET VII: HISTORY MATTERS

Sir John Templeton also observed that 'This time is different' were the four most dangerous words in investing. Or as J.K. Galbraith said, the markets are characterized by

> Extreme brevity of the financial memory. In consequence, financial disaster is quickly forgotten. In further consequence, when the same or closely similar circumstances occur again, sometimes in a few years, they are hailed by a new, often youthful, and always supremely self-confident generation as a brilliantly innovative discovery in the financial and larger economic world. There can be few fields of human endeavor in which history counts for so little as in the world of finance.

Perhaps my favorite quotation on the lack of historical appreciation in finance comes from Jeremy Grantham who, when asked 'Do you think we will learn anything from this turmoil?' responded,

> We will learn an enormous amount in the very short term, quite a bit in the medium term and absolutely nothing in the long term. That would be the historical precedent.

Our industry often appears to be devoid of any appreciation of what has happened in the past. I often think that we would all be well served if, instead of studying the esoteric and complex maths of Black and Scholes and Itô's Lemma, those working in finance were required to study the history of what has gone before.

Strangely enough, the CFA ensures that its charter holders are conversant in the mechanics of DCF, and can recite the joys of VaR, but notably absent is a chapter (let alone a module) on the lessons offered by financial history. As Ben Graham argued, 'Prudence suggests that he [the investor] have an adequate idea of stock market history, in terms particularly of the major fluctuations . . . With this background he may be in a position to form some worthwhile judgement of the attractiveness or dangers . . . of the market.'

Nowhere is an appreciation of history more important than in understanding bubbles. As I have written before, we have long been proponents of the Kindleberger/Minsky framework for analyzing bubbles. Essentially, this model breaks a bubble's rise and fall into five phases, as shown in the following:

Displacement → Credit creation → Euphoria →
Critical stage/Financial distress → Revulsion

- **Displacement: The birth of a boom.**
  Displacement is generally an exogenous shock that triggers the creation of profit opportunities in some sectors, while closing down profit availability in other sectors. As long as the opportunities created are greater than those that get shut down, investment and production will pick up to exploit these new opportunities. Investment in both financial and physical assets is likely to occur. Effectively we are witnessing the birth of a boom.

- **Credit creation: The nurturing of a bubble.**
  Just as fire can't grow without oxygen, so a boom needs liquidity to feed on. Minsky argued that monetary expansion and credit creation are largely endogenous to the system. That is to say, not only can money be created by existing banks but also by the formation of new banks, the development of new credit instruments and the expansion of personal credit outside the banking system.

- **Euphoria.**
  Everyone starts to buy into the new era. Prices are seen as only capable of ever going up. Traditional valuation standards are abandoned, and new measures are introduced to justify the current price. A wave of overoptimism and overconfidence is unleashed, leading people to overestimate the gains, underestimate the risks and generally think they can control the situation.

- **Critical stage/Financial distress.**
  The critical stage is often characterized by insiders cashing out, and is rapidly followed by financial distress, in which the excess leverage that has been built up during the boom becomes a major problem. Fraud also often emerges during this stage of the bubble's life.

- **Revulsion.**
  This is the final stage of a bubble's life cycle. Investors are so scarred by the events in which they participated that they can no longer bring themselves to participate in the market at all. This results in bargain basement asset prices.

As Table 1.1 shows, the key features of bubbles are unnervingly similar. While the specific details of each bubble are unique, the overall patterns are essentially the same. Surely learning to spot these signs would be a worthwhile pursuit.

TENET VIII: BE SKEPTICAL

In trying to write down the list of tenets that form the approach I follow, it was sometimes hard to work out where one tenet began and another ended. Being skeptical was one of those that seemed to be covered by other tenets, but I felt it was worthy of examination in its own right. One of my non-finance heros (Bruce Springsteen) once remarked that 'Blind faith in anything will get you killed'. I share this view on the dangers of lack of critical thinking.

Table 1.1 The pattern of historical bubbles

Event	South Sea bubble (1710–1720)	First British railway boom (1845)	US 1873 railway boom	1920s US equity bubble
Displacement	Profit from conversion of government debt, supposed monopoly on trade with Spanish Americas	End of depression, new means of transport	End of the Civil War, settlement of the war	Decade of fast growth, end of WWI, rapid expansion of mass production
Smart money response	Insiders buy up debt in advance of conversion	Build a railroad	Construction of government subsidized railroads	Expansion of supply of new shares, creation of new closed end funds
Substaining the bubble	Development of the coffee house network for speculation	?	Additional railroad charters	Regional exchanges, growth of margin accounts and broker loans
Authoritative blessing	Government approval, royal involvement	Government approval of each railroad	Henry Varnum Poor and Charles Frances Adams	Blessing from Coolridge, Hoover, Mellon and Irving Fisher
Swindle/Fraud	Ponzi scheme	George Hudson paying dividends out of capital (Ponzi scheme)	?	Russel Snyder and Samuel Insull buying binge and debt mountain
Political reaction	Ex-post facto punishing of the directors, restrictions of the use of corporate form	Reform of accounting standards, rules passed so that dividends must be paid out of earnings not capital	?	Glass-Steagall Act, creation of the SEC, the holding company act

Table 1.1 *(Continued)*

Event	1960s conglomerate mergers boom	1980s Japanese land and equity bubbles	TMT bubble	Credit/Risk bubble
Displacement	Two decades of rising stock markets, the joy of growth investing	Financial liberalization, monetary easing	Widespread acceptance of the internet, strong growth and monetary easing	Low rates, rising house prices, Great Moderation
Smart money response	Emergence of professional conglomerates	Zaitech	Aggressive growth funds, stock options and IPO boom	Any and all kinds of leverage
Sustaining the bubble	Stock swaps to create apparent earnings growth	Cross shareholders, latent asset value, PKO in '87	Pro forma earnings, new valuation measures, buybacks	New derivative structures — CDOs, CDOs squared, new mortgage products, buybacks
Authoritative blessing	McGeorge Bundy	Nomura calls for 80,000 by 1995	Greenspan	Greenspan, Bernanke, Bush
Swindle/Fraud	National Student Marketing Corp.	Recruit Cosmo, Bubble lady	Enron, WorldCom, Tyco etc	Mark to model/myth, Madoff, Stanford
Political reaction	Reform of accounting practice and the Williams Act	?	Sarbanes Oxley	??

Source: SG Global Strategy research.

Over the years, I have had the privilege of knowing some of the best investors (judged by both their decisions and their results). One of the hallmarks they share is a healthy degree of skepticism. Indeed, I would go as far as to say that they have a very different default when it comes to investing relative to the vast majority of fund managers. Their default option is non-ownership. They need to be convinced of the merits of an investment. This provides an inbuilt skepticism to their approach. They aren't willing to simply take things at face value. Their desire to understand the potential downside risks ensures that they focus on what could go wrong, rather than dreaming of what could go right.

Most fund managers (especially those engaged in the relative performance derby) are more concerned with tracking error than skepticism. Their default is: Why shouldn't I own this investment? This short-circuits the skeptical inquiries that mark out those top investors.

Skepticism is also vital for those of us whose work regularly takes them in the dark side (aka the short side). As mentioned in Tenet IV, I have no problem with being net short if that is where the opportunities lie. Indeed, I think short selling should be encouraged, not outlawed. As I have written many times before, the short sellers I know are among the most fundamentally oriented investors I have ever met. They take their analysis very seriously (as they should, since their downside is effectively unlimited). There can be no substitute for independent thinking, solid research and a healthy degree of skepticism.

TENET IX: BE TOP-DOWN AND BOTTOM-UP

I started my career in finance as an economist (not something I admit in public very often; in fact I started out as an econometrician, which is possibly even worse). However, one of the few things I learned from my years in the wilderness was that top-down and bottom-up are largely inseparable (much like value and growth — they aren't mutually exclusive; as Buffett said, they are joined at the hip).

In his book on value investing, Marty Whitman says 'Graham and Dodd view macrofactors . . . as crucial to the analysis of a corporate security. Value investors, however, believe that macrofactors are irrelevant.' If this is the case then I am very proud to say I am a Graham and Dodd fundamentalist.

While stock selection is best approached from the bottom-up, ignoring the top-down can be extraordinarily expensive. The last year has been a perfect example of why understanding the top-down can benefit and inform the bottom-up. The last 12 months have been unusual for value investors as two clear camps emerged from their normally more homogeneous whole.

A schism over financials has split value investors into two diametrically opposed groups. The optimistic/bottom-up view was typified by Richard Pzena. In his Q1 2008 quarterly report he wrote:

A new fear has permeated conventional investment thinking: the massive leveraging-up of the recent past has gone too far and its unwinding will permanently hobble the global financial system. This view sees Bear Stearns as just one casualty in a gathering wave that has already claimed many US subprime mortgage originators along with several non-US financial institutions and will cause countless others to fail. And it sees the earnings power of those that survive as being permanently impaired.

The obvious question then is, which scenario is more logical: the extreme outlook described above, given the long period of easy credit extended to unqualified individuals? Or the scenario of a typical credit cycle that will work its way out as other post-excess crises have, and without impairing the long-term ROEs of the survivors? We believe the latter.

The alternative view (pessimistic, top-down informed) is well summed up by Steven Romick of First Pacific Advisors in a recent interview in Value Investor Insight:

VII: Has your negative general view on the prospects for financial services stocks changed at all?

SR: We believe in reversion to the mean, so it can make a lot of sense to invest in a distressed sector when you find good businesses whose public shares trade inexpensively relative to their earnings in a more normal environment. But that strategy lately has helped to lead many excellent investors to put capital to work too early in financials. Our basic feeling is that margins and returns on capital generated by financial institutions in the decade through 2006 were unrealistically high. 'Normal' profitability and valuation multiples are not going to be what they were during that time, given more regulatory oversight, less leverage (and thus capital to lend), higher funding costs, stricter underwriting standards, less demand and less esoteric and excessively profitable products.

Essentially, the difference between these two camps comes down to an appreciation of the importance of the bursting of the credit bubble. Those who understood the impact of the bursting of such a bubble didn't go near financials (and are generally still not prepared to engage in knife-catching in this sector). Those who focused more (and in some cases exclusively) on the bottom-up just saw cheapness.

It often pays to remember the wise words of Jean-Marie Eveillard, 'Sometimes, what matters is not so much how low the odds are that circumstances would turn quite negative, what matters more is what the consequences would be if that happens.'

As mentioned previously, while we can't predict we can prepare. The credit bubble wasn't a black swan, although we might not have been able to forecast when its demise would occur, we could at least prepare for its passing on by avoiding credit bubble-related stocks such as financials and housebuilders, for instance.

The bottom-up can also inform the top-down. As Ben Graham pointed out, 'True bargain issues have repeatedly become scarce in bull markets . . . Perhaps one could even have determined whether the market level was getting too high or too low by counting the number of issues selling below working capital value. When such opportunities have virtually disappeared, past experience indicates that investors should have taken themselves out of the stock market and plunged up to their necks in US Treasury bills.'

Another example of the complementary nature of top-down and bottom-up viewpoints is offered by Seth Klarman. In his insightful book, *Margin of Safety*, Klarman points out that the inflationary environment can have dramatic consequences for value investors:

Trends in inflation or deflation also cause business values to fluctuate. That said, value investing can work very well in an inflationary environment. If for 50 cents you buy a dollar of value in the form of an asset, such as natural resource properties or real estate, which increases in value with inflation, a fifty-cent investment today can result in the realization of value appreciably greater than one dollar. In an inflationary environment, however, investors may become somewhat careless. As long as assets are rising in value, it would appear attractive to relax one's standards and purchase $1 of assets, not for 50 cents, but for 70 or 80 cents (or perhaps even $1.10). Such laxity could prove costly, however, in the event that inflation comes to be anticipated by most investors, who respond by bidding up security prices. A subsequent slowdown in the rate of inflation could cause a price decline.

In a deflationary environment assets tend to decline in value. Buying a dollar's worth of assets for 50 cents may not be a bargain if the asset value is dropping. Historically investors have found attractive opportunities in companies with substantial 'hidden assets', such as an overfunded pension fund, real estate carried on the balance sheet below market value, or a profitable finance subsidiary that could be sold at a significant gain. Amidst a broad-based decline in business and asset values, however, some hidden assets become less valuable and in some cases may become hidden liabilities. A decline in the stock market will reduce the value of pension fund assets; previously overfunded plans may become underfunded. Real estate carried on companies' balance sheets at historical cost may no longer be undervalued. Overlooked subsidiaries that were once hidden jewels may lose their lustre.

The possibility of sustained decreases in business value is a dagger at the heart of value investing (and is not a barrel of laughs for other investment approaches either). Value investors place great faith in the principle of assessing value and then buying at a discount. If value is subject to considerable erosion, then how large a discount is sufficient?

Should investors worry about the possibility that business value may decline? Absolutely. Should they do anything about it? There are three responses that might be effective. First, since investors cannot predict when values will rise or fall, valuation should always be performed conservatively, giving considerable weight to worst-case liquidation value as well as to other methods. Second, investors fearing deflation could demand a greater than usual discount between price and underlying value in order to make new investments or to hold current positions. This means that normally selective investors would probably let even more pitches than usual go by.

Finally, the prospect of asset deflation places a heightened importance on the timeframe of investments and on the presence of a catalyst for the realization of underlying value. In a deflationary environment, if you cannot tell whether or when you will realize underlying value, you may not want to get involved at all. If underlying value is realized in the near-term directly for the benefit of shareholders, however, the longer-term forces that could cause value to diminish become moot.

Thus, neither top-down nor bottom-up has a monopoly on insight. Both perspectives have something to offer the open-minded investor.

TENET X: TREAT YOUR CLIENTS LIKE YOU WOULD YOURSELF

The final tenet of my creed takes us almost a full circle back to the aim of investing (which for those with both pachyderm-like memories and the extraordinary stamina required to make it thus far through this chapter, will recall was where we started).

One of the most useful questions I think a fund manager can ask is: Would I do this with my own money? All too often those charged with the stewardship of other people's money seem to think that this gives them licence to behave in an odd fashion (true of both fund managers and the corporate executives charged with running companies).

John Bogle put it well when he said our industry has ceased to be a profession and has become a business. This is a lamentable state of affairs. When marketing men run investment firms, the result will be the wrong fund at just the wrong time. Witness the surge in tech funds in the late 1990s, or the rise of commodity funds in more recent years. I have long argued that we need a version of the Hippocratic Oath in finance with an overt promise to 'first, do no harm'.

Paul Wilmott and Emanuel Derman recently proposed the following as the 'Modelers' Hippocratic Oath':

I will remember that I didn't make the world, and it doesn't satisfy my equations.

Though I will use models boldly to estimate value, I will not be overly impressed by mathematics.

I will never sacrifice reality for elegance without explaining why I have done so.

Nor will I give the people who use my model false comfort about its accuracy. Instead, I will make explicit its assumptions and oversights.

I understand that my work may have enormous effects on society and the economy, many of them beyond my comprehension.

Instead of trying to maximize assets under management, many of the best investors have chosen to deliberately limit the size of their funds, so as not to reduce their ability to deliver returns. Of course, this is anathema to the fund supermarkets, but it strikes me as the only way to sensibly approach investing. As Jean-Marie Eveillard said, 'I would rather lose half my clients than lose half my client's money.'

Incentives can be aligned without too much difficulty. For instance, buy-side analysts should be paid on a (say) three-year view of overall performance of the fund at which they work. This prevents them gaming the system and insisting on having positions in the portfolio. I would also suggest that analysts should be generalists rather than specialists. This allows them flexibility to assess different opportunities in different areas, but ensures that a consistent framework is applied. However, here I am straying towards process rather than philosophy, which is the subject of this thesis.

Similarly, I am always happiest investing when I know the manager has a sizeable stake in the fund alongside my own, simply because this helps to ensure that he asks himself the question with which I started this section on a regular basis.

Managers who follow the kind of creed I have outlined earlier will also need to select their clients with care. Having clients who truly understand the way you invest is vital, after all there is little point in trying to follow a patient strategy if your capital is pulled at just the wrong moment. Using precommitment devices such as lock-ins makes sense in this context.

CONCLUSION

This is perhaps one of the most personal chapters I have ever written. It exposes my beliefs about the way in which investment should be approached. I have tried to avoid a discussion of process — not because I believe it to be unimportant (in fact nothing could be further from the truth), but rather because I wanted to explore the philosophical beliefs that lie at the very core of the approach I follow.

Exposing one's beliefs can be a risky move, but just as sunlight is the best disinfectant, so I think exposing beliefs to critique is a useful exercise. Open and honest debate can often produce superior results. It is in this spirit that I have tried to explain the way I approach investing. It certainly isn't the only way we could approach the problem, but it is the way that makes the most sense to me.

1.12.1 The Ten Tenets of Investing

Tenet I: Value, value, value
Tenet II: Be contrarian
Tenet III: Be patient
Tenet IV: Be unconstrained
Tenet V: Don't forecast
Tenet VI: Cycles matter
Tenet VII: History matters
Tenet VIII: Be skeptical
Tenet IX: Be top-down and bottom-up
Tenet X: Treat your clients as you would treat yourself

2

Clear and Present Danger:
The Trinity of Risk[1]

Despite risk appearing to be one of finance's favorite four-letter words, it remains finance's most misunderstood concept. Risk isn't a number, it is a concept or a notion. From my perspective, risk equates to what Ben Graham called a 'permanent loss of capital'. Three primary (although interrelated) sources of such danger can be identified: valuation risk, business/earnings risk, and balance sheet/financial risk. Rather than running around obsessing on the pseudoscience of risk management, investors should concentrate on understanding the nature of this trinity of risks.

- Value investing is the only investment approach (of which I am aware) that truly puts risk management at the very heart of the process. Ben Graham was deeply critical of modern finance's obsession with standard deviation (and I'm sure he would have laughed out loud at VaR). He argued that investors should concentrate on the dangers of 'permanent loss of capital.'

- Graham went on to suggest at least three broad risks that could result in such a loss. We have termed these: valuation risk, business/earnings risk, and balance sheet/financial risk. Valuation risk is perhaps the most obvious of our trinity. Buying an asset that is expensive means that you are reliant upon all the good news being delivered (and then some). There is no margin of safety in such stocks.

- Some markets display more valuation risk than others. For instance, the UK market is trading on an 11× Graham and Dodd PE, and only 30% of stocks in the UK have G&D PEs >16×. In the US, the G&D PE for the market is 16×, and some 52% of stocks are on G&D PEs >16×. However, valuation risk is far less concerning than a year or two ago.

- Business or earnings risk is considerably more worrying at the current juncture. As Graham said 'real risk is . . . the danger of a loss of quality and earnings power through economic changes or deterioration in management.' The markets certainly seem to be implying that business risk is high. The dividend swap markets are suggesting a near 50% decline in European dividends, a 40% decline in UK dividends, and a 21% decline in US dividends! The challenge to investors is to assess whether changes in earnings power are temporary or permanent. The former are, of course, opportunities; the latter are value traps.

---

[1]This article appeared in *Mind Matters* on 27 January 2009. Copyright © 2009 by The Société Générale Group. All rights reserved. The material discussed was accurate at the time of publication.

- Balance sheet/financing risk is the last of our triumvirate. As Graham noted: 'The purpose of balance sheet analysis is to detect . . . the presence of financial weakness that may detract from the investment merit of an issue.' In general, we have found that these risks get ignored by investors during the good times, but in a credit constrained environment they suddenly reappear on the agenda. We would suggest that rather than vascillating between neglect and obsession with respect to the balance sheet, a more even approach may well generate results.

Value investing is the only investment approach that puts risk management at the very heart of the process. The margin of safety is nothing if not a form of risk management against errors and bad luck.

Ben Graham warned that risk couldn't be measured in a neat easy way. He certainly didn't equate risk with standard deviation, and I'm sure he would have no time for VaR at all. Rather, Graham saw risk as the 'permanent loss of capital.'

For several years I have argued that the permanent loss of capital can be split into three (interrelated) sets of risks: valuation risk, business/earnings risk, and balance sheet/financing risk. Let's take each of these in turn and see how they apply to the current situation.

VALUATION RISK

As Graham wrote, 'The danger in . . . growth stock(s) [is that] for such favored issues the market has a tendency to set prices that will not be adequately protected by a conservative projection of future earnings.' In other words, buying expensive stocks leaves you vulnerable to disappointment.

Of course, given the way in which markets have declined over the last year, valuation risk has become less of an issue. That is not to say it is yet absent. As Figure 2.1 shows, the US equity market is currently just below 'fair value' — not yet at truly bargain basement prices. I have no idea whether this major recession will take us to truly bargain valuations, but serious bear markets have normally only ended when we are trading on 10×10-year moving average earnings. This is consistent with the S&P 500 at 500!

Figure 2.1   S&P 500 Graham and Dodd PE
Source: SG Global Strategy research.

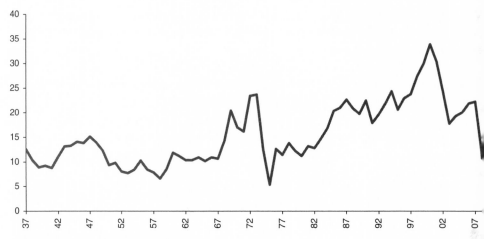

Figure 2.2   UK Graham and Dodd PE
Source: SG Global Strategy research.

In late November, 2008, I was able to argue that the US market was trading on the cheap side of fair value. However, a 25% rally between late November and year end shows just how the short term can make a mockery of the long term on occasion.

Other markets continue to show more valuation support than the US from a top-down perspective. For instance, both the UK and Europe are currently sitting on much more attractive multiples. As Figure 2.2 shows, the UK market is sitting on just under 11×.

This top-down valuation work is supported by looking at the percentage of stocks trading at Graham and Dodd PEs greater than 16×. You may well ask why 16×? The answer as ever lies in the writings of Graham who opined:

> We would suggest that about 16 times is as high a price as can be paid in an investment purchase of a common stock . . . Although this rule is of necessity arbitrary in its nature, it is not entirely so. Investment presupposes demonstrable value, and the typical common stock's value can be demonstrated only by means of an established, i.e. an average, earnings power. But it is difficult to see how average earnings of less than 6% upon the market price could ever be considered as vindicating that price.

Figure 2.3 shows the percentage of stocks (in the large cap universe) that are currently sitting on Graham and Dodd PEs of greater than 16×. In the US, still over half the stocks find themselves in this position, better value can be found in the UK and Europe where only around one-third of stocks are still on G&D PE > 16×. Interestingly, it is in Japan where we find the highest percentage of stocks still trading on high PEs, some 57%!

Thus, despite market declines valuation risk is not yet absent from markets. We continue to drip-feed cash into deep value opportunities and sources of cheap insurance.

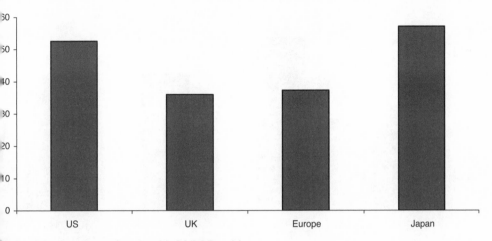

Figure 2.3 Percentage of stocks with G&D PEs > **16×**
Source: SG Global Strategy research.

BUSINESS/EARNINGS RISK

The second source of risk from our perspective concerns business and earnings risk. As Graham put it:

> Real investment risk is measured not by the percent that a stock may decline in price in relation to the general market in a given period, but by the danger of a loss of quality and earnings power through economic changes or deterioration in management.

In an environment which is increasingly being acknowledged as the worst since the Great Depression, a loss of 'earnings power through economic changes' must be a concern for investors. Graham warned that markets were 'governed more by their current earnings than by their long-term average. This fact accounts in good part for the wide fluctuations in common-stock prices, which largely (though by no means invariably) parallel the changes in their earnings between good years and bad.'

Graham went on:

> Obviously, the stock market is quite irrational in thus varying its valuation of a company proportionately with the temporary changes in reported profits. A private business might easily earn twice as much in a boom year as in poor times, but its owner would never think of correspondingly marking up or down the value of his capital investment.

The challenge facing investors in this environment is to assess whether any changes in earnings power are temporary or permanent. The former represent opportunities, the latter value traps.

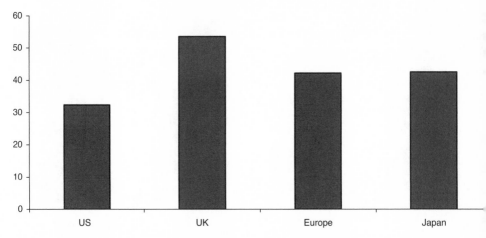

Figure 2.4   Percentage of stocks with current EPS > **2× 10-year average EPS**
Source: SG Global Strategy research.

Keep an eye on the ratio of current EPS to average 10-year EPS. Stocks which look 'cheap' based on current earnings, but not on average earnings, are the ones that investors should be especially aware of, as they run a greater risk of being the sort of stock where the apparent cheapness is removed by earnings falling rather than prices rising.

Figure 2.4 shows the percentage of stocks in the large cap universe that have current EPS of at least twice 10-year average EPS. This serves as our proxy for earnings risk. In the US only one-third of stocks find themselves in this situation (as befits the country first into this crisis). The UK comes out as the worst on this measure, with 54% of stocks having current EPS of at least twice 10-year average EPS. In Europe and Japan, 42% of stocks are in this position. It appears to us that earnings and business risk are far more absent in these markets. The good news is that, given the lower valuations mentioned above, this may already be partially discounted.

BALANCE SHEET/FINANCIAL RISK

The third of our unholy trinity of risks is balance sheet/financial risk. As Graham opines, 'The purpose of balance-sheet analysis is to detect . . . the presence of financial weakness that may detract from the investment merit of an issue.'

Investors tend to ignore balance sheet and financial risk at the height of booms. They get distracted by earnings, and how these cyclically high earnings cover interest payments. Only when earnings start to crumble do investors turn their attention back to the balance sheet. Similarly leverage is used to turn little profits into big profits during the good times, and many investors seem to forget that leverage works in reverse as well, effectively a big profit can rapidly become a loss during a downswing.

There are lots of ways of gauging balance sheet risk. Our colleagues in the quant team have long argued that the Merton Model and distance to default provide a useful measure of these dimensions. Being a simple and old-fashioned soul, I turn to a measure that has served me well in the past during periods of balance sheet stress: good old Altman's Z.

Altman's Z score was designed in 1968 to predict bankruptcy using five simple ratios.

$$Z = 1.2X_1 + 1.4X_2 + 3.3X_3 + 0.6X_4 + 0.999X_5$$

X_1 = Working Capital/Total Assets. Measures liquid assets in relation to the size of the
      company.

X_2 = Retained Earnings/Total Assets. Measures profitability that reflects the company's
      age and earning power.

X_3 = Earnings Before Interest and Taxes/Total Assets. Measures operating efficiency
      apart from tax and leveraging factors. It recognizes operating earnings as being
      important to long-term viability.

X_4 = Market Value of Equity/Book Value of Total Liabilities. Adds market dimension
      that can show up security price fluctuation as a possible red flag.

X_5 = Sales/Total Assets. Standard measure for turnover.

A Z score below 1.8 is considered a good indication of future problems. While only a first step, I have often found this measure useful for flagging up potentially troubling situations. Figure 2.5 shows the percentage of large cap firms across countries which have Altman Z scores below 1.8. The measure obviously won't work for financials or utilities so they have been excluded from our sample.

Roughly speaking, we find very similar levels of balance sheet risk across countries. Somewhere between 20 and 25% of companies appear to have Z scores below 1.8, suggesting a high probability of financial distress.

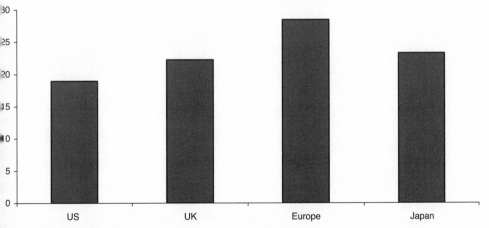

Figure 2.5   Percentage of stocks with Altman Z scored <**1.8**
Source: SG Global Strategy research.

PUTTING IT ALL TOGETHER

These three elements (intertwined as they are) can all lead to a permanent loss of capital. Ultimately, I would argue that risk is really a notion or a concept not a number. Indeed the use of pseudoscience in risk management has long been a rant of mine.

3

The Psychology of Bear Markets[1]

The mental barriers to effective decision-making in bear markets are as many and varied as those that plague rationality during bull markets. However, in bear markets the primary role of emotion is particularly pronounced as the resulting fear and shock short circuit more logical analysis. Experiments have shown that those that can't feel fear behave more rationally in the face of loss than those who can. Perhaps many of the extremes we experience during our moments of both euphoria and revulsion could be avoided if only we heed the words of King Solomon's advisers 'This too, shall pass'.

- It is a cliché that markets are driven by fear and greed. However, it is also disturbingly close to the truth. Having spent the best part of a decade exploring the psychology of bull markets, it makes a refreshing change to examine the drivers of bear market behavior.
- Fear seems to lie at the heart of the psychology of bear markets. The bad news for us humans is that within the brain emotion appears to have primacy over cognitive functions. Our brains consist of two different (although interconnected) systems. One is a fast and dirty decision maker (the X-system), the other is more logical but slower (the C-system).
- The X-system's output is often unchecked (or at least checked only too late) by the C-system. For instance, if I were to place a glass box containing a snake on the table in front of you, and asked you to move as close as you could to the box, you would jump backward if the snake reared up — even if you aren't afraid of snakes. The reason for this is that the X-system 'recognized' a threat and forced the body to react, all of which was done before the C-system had a chance to point out the protection offered by the glass box. Effectively from an evolutionary standpoint a rapid response to fear carried a very low cost to a false positive, relative to the potentially fatal cost of a false negative.
- While such an approach may have kept us alive, it doesn't necessarily work in our favor when thinking about financial markets. In a fascinating experiment Shiv et al. show that when taking risk is rewarded over the long term, players who can't feel fear (due to a very specific form of brain damage) perform much better than the rest of us. Shiv et al. also show that the longer the game goes on, the worse people's performance becomes.
- The parallels of the Shiv et al. game with bear markets are (I hope) obvious. The evidence suggests that it is outright fear that drives people to ignore bargains when they are available in the market, if they have previously suffered a loss. The longer they find themselves in this position the worse their decision making appears to become.

- Investors should consider the Buddhist approach to time. That is to say, the past is history and the future is a mystery, and so we must focus on the present. The decision to invest or not should be a function of the current situation (the value on offer) and not governed by prior experiences (or indeed our future hopes). Perhaps we would all do well to remember the sage words of King Solomon's advisers when charged to find an expression that would be 'true and appropriate in all times and situations', that 'This too, shall pass'.

After a decade of exploring the psychology of bull markets, it makes a refreshing change to able to think about the psychology that drives behavior in bear markets. Of course, many of the same biases that lead us to extrapolate the good times at the peak lead us to do the same on the downside.

We seem to constantly fail to remember the wisdom of King Solomon (or rather his advisers). As Abraham Lincoln relayed the story:

> Solomon once charged his wise men to invent him a sentence, to be ever in view, which should be true and appropriate in all times and situations. They presented him with the words 'And this, too, shall pass away'. How much it expresses! How chastening in the hour of pride. How consoling in the depths of affliction.

If only we were capable of heeding these words!

Unfortunately, many of the biases we face seem to stem from the X-system (the automatic part of our brain's processing capabilities). As such they are outside of our conscious awareness and therefore can sometimes (indeed one could say, often) go unchecked by the more logical C-system.

FEAR AND BEAR MARKETS

Of particular note when considering bear markets is an insightful study by Shiv *et al.* (2005). They asked players to participate in the following game. At the start of the game you are given $20 and told the following — the game will last 20 rounds. At the start of each round you will be asked if you would like to invest. If you say yes then the cost will be $1. A fair coin will then be flipped. If it comes up heads you will receive $2.50 back, if it comes up tails then you will lose your $1.

Now there are two things we know about this game. Firstly, obviously it is optimal to invest in all rounds due to the asymmetric nature of the payoff (expected value is $1.25, giving a total expected value to the game of $25). In fact there is only a 13% chance that you end up with total earnings of less than $20 (i.e. the return you achieve if you don't invest at all and just keep the initial endowment). The second thing we know about this game is that the outcome in a prior round shouldn't impact your decision to invest in the next round — after all the coin has no memory.

Now cast your eye over Figure 3.1. It shows the percentage of time people chose to invest depending upon the outcome in the previous round. As you can see three groups of players were used in the experiment. The black bars (target patients) represent a very unusual group. They have a very specific form of brain damage;[2] effectively these individuals can no longer feel fear. The light gray bars (normals) are people like you and I (ostensibly without any brain damage). The dark gray bars (control patients) are those with brain damage in other parts of the brain not related to the processing of emotion (and fear).

---

[2]Technically they have lesions on the orbitofrontal cortex, the amygdala or the right insular or somatosensory cortex — all areas associated with emotional processing in the X-system.

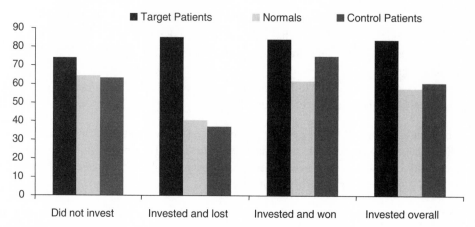

Figure 3.1 Percentage of decisions to invest as a function of outcome in the previous round
Source: Shiv *et al.* (2005).

It is the second group of three bars to which I wish to draw your attention. This is the percentage of time that players chose to invest after a round in which they had invested and lost. The first group of players — those who can't feel fear — behave quite optimally, investing around 85% of the time after they have suffered a loss. However, look at the other two groups. They display seriously suboptimal behavior. In fact, so bad is the pain/fear of losing even $1 that these groups invested less than 40% of the time after a round in which they had suffered a loss!

AS TIME GOES PAST

Equally (if not more disturbing) is the complete lack of learning that both 'normals' and 'patient controls' display over the course of the game. Figure 3.2 shows the overall percentage of time that the various groups of players chose to invest broken down into four groups of five games. Of course, if players were rational and learned from their experience then these lines would slope upwards from left to right (i.e. the longer the game went on, the more they would invest). Unfortunately, for both 'normals' and 'patient controls' the lines slope downwards from left to right — that is to say, the longer the game went on, the less they decided to invest. They were getting worse at the game as time went past.

The parallels with bear markets are (I hope) obvious. The evidence above suggests that it is outright fear that drives people to ignore bargains when they are available in the market, if they have previously suffered a loss. The longer they find themselves in this position the worse their decision making appears to become.

Of course, this game is designed so that taking risk yields good results. If the game were reversed and taking risk ended in poor outcomes, the 'normals' would outperform the players who can't feel fear. However, I would argue that the former is a better description of the current environment than the latter. When markets are cheap, the odds are good for high future returns. But, of course, markets are cheap because of all the bad news we are currently receiving.

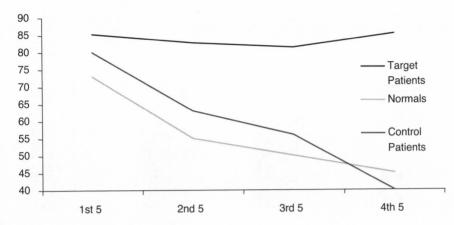

Figure 3.2 Percentage investing over time
Source: Shiv *et al.* (2005).

THE IMPACT OF BRAIN DRAIN

The fact that time seems to drain the ability to think rationally fits with a lot of the work done looking at the psychology of self-control. Baumeister (2003) argues that self-control (effectively our ability to hold our emotions in check) is like a muscle — too much use leads to exhaustion. He concludes his survey of the field by highlighting the key findings of his research:

> When self-esteem is threatened, people become upset and lose their capacity to regulate themselves . . . when self-regulation fails people may become increasingly self-defeating in various ways, such as taking immediate pleasures instead of delayed rewards. Self-regulation appears to depend on limited resources that operate like strength or energy, and so people can only regulate themselves to a limited extent.

People tend to display the ability for self-regulation in varying degrees. In the past I have administered a test known as the cognitive reflection test[3] (CRT) to measure how easy each of us finds it to override our X-system. The CRT is made up of three questions.

1. A bat and a ball together cost $1.10. The bat costs a dollar more than the ball. How much does the ball cost?
2. It takes 5 machines 5 minutes to make 5 widgets. How long will it take 100 machines to make 100 widgets?
3. In a lake there is a patch of lily pads. The patch doubles in size every day. If it takes 48 days for the patch to cover the entire lake, how long would it take for the patch to cover half the lake?

---

[3]This test was originally created by Shane Frederik of MIT.

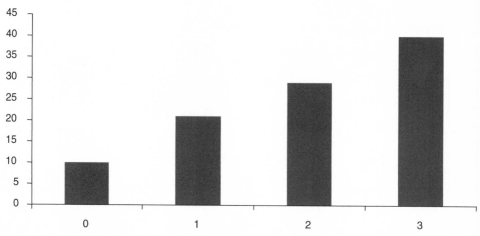

Figure 3.3   Percentage of CRT questions correctly answered
Source: SG Equity research.

Each question has an obvious but unfortunately incorrect answer (the X-system response), and also a less obvious but nonetheless correct answer (the logical C-system solution). Because X-system is a 'satisfier' rather than a 'maximizer', it searches for solutions that look approximately correct. If left unchecked it provides these as the 'true' answers. If one engages in self-regulation, then the C-system is activated to check the output and override it where necessary.

I have given over 700 fund managers and analysts these three questions (among many others) over the years. Figure 3.3 shows the percentage of respondents by the number of CRT questions successfully answered. Only 40% of fund managers managed to get all three questions right. Effectively 60% didn't engage in sufficient self-regulation!

A recent study by Sweldens and colleagues (De Laughe *et al.* 2008) studied the same game that is outlined earlier, but measured people on the basis of their degree of reliance upon their X-system.[4] If the depletion of resources is a problem, then those who rely on their X-system more should suffer poorer decision-making when they have been forced to use up their store of self-regulatory ability. In order to achieve this, one group of players was subjected to a Stroop test. The Stroop test will be familiar to fans of Brain Training games — although they may not know its name. It presents the names of colors, and players have to name the color in which the name of the color is written, rather than the name of the color. Thus the word RED may appear in blue ink, and the correct response is blue. It thus takes concentration and willpower to complete the Stroop test.

---

[4]They used a self-report approach. So people were measured on the basis of how much they agreed or disagreed with eight statements such as 'I tend to use my heart as a guide for my actions', 'I like to reply on my intuitive impressions', 'I don't have very good sense of intuition', etc. rather than a more clinical approach such as the CRT.

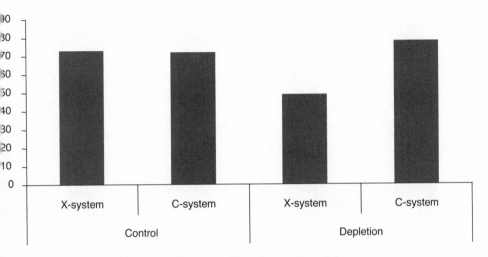

Figure 3.4 Percentage of time invested by processing style and test condition
Source: De Langhe *et al.* (2008).

Figure 3.4 shows the overall percentage of time which people choose to invest depending upon their cognitive processing style and whether or not they had to complete the Stroop test. In the control condition (i.e. without the Stroop test), both those who relied on X- and C-system processing performed in the same fashion. They invested around 70% of the time (still distinctly suboptimally). The results were very different when self-regulation was depleted. Those with a very strong reliance on their C-system continued to do well, investing 78% of the time. However, those who relied heavily on their X-system suffered particularly badly. They invested only 49% of the time!

Given that this kind of behavior might encompass up to 60% of fund managers, it isn't surprising that many professional investors don't feel inclined to accept the bargains being offered by Mr. Market at the moment.

THE BLANK SLATE

Investors should consider trying to adopt the Buddhist approach to time. That is to say, the past is gone and can't be changed, the future is unknown, and so we must focus on the present. The decision to invest or not should be a function of the current situation (from my perspective the degree of value on offer) not governed by our prior experiences (or indeed our future hopes). However, this blank slate is mentally very hard to achieve. Our brains seem to be wired to focus on the short term and to fear loss in an extreme fashion. These mental hurdles are barriers to sensible investment decision-making in a bear market.

4

The Behavioral Stumbling Blocks to Value Investing[1]

The fact that value outperforms over the long term is not new news. Yet despite this, there are relatively few 'true' value managers. This chapter seeks to explore the behavioral stumbling blocks that conspire to prevent us doing what we know to be right. Loss aversion, present bias, herding, availability and overconfidence are just a few of the hurdles that must be overcome to exploit value opportunities.

- Psychologists argue that knowledge and behavior are not one and the same thing. That is to say, we sometimes do what we know to be wrong. For instance, the knowledge that safe sex can reduce the risk of HIV/AIDS doesn't always translate into the use of a condom. The same is true in other fields; simply knowing that value outperforms over the long term isn't enough to persuade everyone to be a value investor.

- Numerous other behavioral stumbling blocks help to explain why value investing is likely to remain a minority sport. Everyone is after the holy grail of investing, a strategy that never loses money! But it doesn't exist. Investing is probabilistic, so losses will occur. However, given our tendency to be loss averse (we dislike losses, more than we like gains) strategies that sometimes see short-term losses will be shunned.

- Long time horizons are integral to value investing. However, they are not natural to humans. Our brains appear to be designed to favor the short term. When faced with the possibility of a short-term gain, we get carried away and forget about the long term. So perhaps Keynes was correct when he wrote: 'Investment based on genuine long-term expectation is so difficult today as to be scarcely practicable.'

- Neuroscientists have found that social pain is felt in exactly the same parts of the brain as real physical pain. Value investing often involves going against the crowd, and hence involves social pain. So value investors are the financial equivalent of masochists.

- The stories associated with value stocks are generally going to be poor. There will be myriad reasons why any given stock is currently out of favor. It is exceptionally difficult to resist these stories, and instead focus on whether the bad news story is already in the price.

---

[1]This article appeared in *Global Equity Strategy* on 29 August 2006. Copyright © 2006 by Dresdner Kleinwort, a Brand of Commerzbank AG. All rights reserved. The material discussed was accurate at the time of publication.

- As is ever the case, overconfidence also rears its ugly head. It is difficult to admit to ourselves (let alone to anyone else) that actually a simple rule can easily outperform us. We all like to think that we can pick stocks, or call asset classes, better than a rule or a model, but the evidence is not supportive of this misplaced, self-aggrandizing view.

- One final word of warning: we all set out with good intentions. However, psychologists have found that we massively overweight our current intentions in the prediction of our future behavior. Thus, as much as we might say, 'OK, now I'm going to be a good value investor', the likelihood of us actually doing so is far, far less than we would like to believe.

KNOWLEDGE ≠ BEHAVIOR

Knowing something to be true isn't always enough to promote changes in behavior. So simply because we can show that value outperforms over the long term, it isn't easy to actually persuade everyone to adopt a value strategy.

A recent paper by Dinkelman *et al.* (2006) makes the difference between knowledge and behavior all too clear. They examined the difference between knowledge of HIV/AIDS and its prevention, and actual sexual behavior (Figure 4.1). For example, 91% of men said they knew that the use of a condom could help to prevent the spread of HIV/AIDS, yet only 70% of them used a condom. Among women the situation was even worse: 92% reported that they knew condoms were useful in preventing HIV/AIDS transmission, but only 63% used them!

If knowledge can't change behavior in these tragic circumstances, why on earth would we expect it to do so in the trivial world of investing?

LOSS AVERSION

Everyone is after the holy grail of investing: a strategy that works all the time. It doesn't exist, so you might as well stop looking, or, even worse, pretending that you have one. The nature of markets is highly probabilistic; uncertainty is central to the act of investing. So nothing is likely to work continuously.

Figure 4.2 shows the percentage of time that value returns are positive on an annual basis (and the percentage of time that they exceed the broad market return). On an annual basis you could reasonably expect value strategies to generate positive absolute returns around 70% of the time (based on MSCI value 1975–2006).

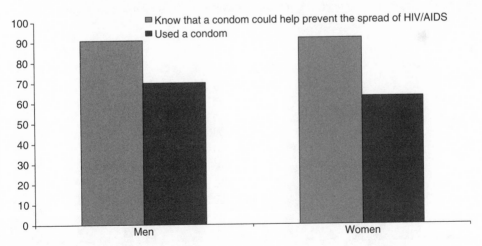

Figure 4.1   Percentage of respondents
Source: Dinkelman *et al.* (2006). DrKW Macro research.

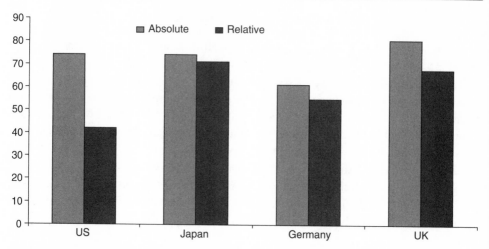

Figure 4.2   Percentage of time value strategies generate positive returns (absolute and relative)
Source: DrKW Macro research.

In 3 years out of every 10, you would see a negative return, and this negative return certainly dissuades many from following such an approach. We all dislike losses much more than we enjoy gains — a phenomenon known as loss aversion.

In many studies, people have been found to dislike losses at least twice as much as they enjoy gains. Consider the following bet: On the toss of a fair coin, if you lose you must pay me $100. What is the minimum you need to win in order to make this bet acceptable to you?

In our survey of over 450 fund managers we found that the average response was $190! So professional fund managers are just as loss averse as the rest of us (see Figure 4.3).

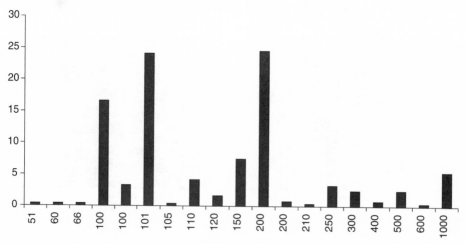

Figure 4.3   Fund managers are just as loss averse as everyone else (frequency %)
Source: DrKW Macro research.

Joel Greenblatt, in his wonderful *Little Book that Beats the Market* details the role that loss aversion plays in deterring investors from following his 'magic formula'. He notes:

> Imagine diligently watching those stocks each day as they do worse than the market average over the course of many months or even years . . . The magic formula portfolio fared poorly relative to the market average in 5 out of every 12 months tested. For full-year period . . . failed to beat the market average once every four years.

So loss aversion certainly plays a pivotal role in dissuading people from becoming value investors.

DELAYED GRATIFICATION AND HARD-WIRING FOR THE SHORT TERM

Not only can value strategies go wrong but they can take time to work. When a value opportunity is exploited there are two ways for it to pay off. For instance, if I buy a significantly undervalued stock, it is possible that everyone else might realize that this is indeed a cheap stock and the price might correct. However, it is also possible that the stock remains undervalued and generates its higher long-run return by continuing to pay a high dividend yield. Both paths are possible, but when a value position is implemented, it is impossible to know *ex-ante* which mechanism will deliver the returns.

This means that value investors must have long time horizons. In our study of value investors we found they had an average holding period of 5 years, whereas the average holding period for a stock on the New York Stock Exchange is only 11 months (see Figures 4.4 and 4.5).

Figure 4.4 Average holding period for a stock on the NYSE (years)
Source: DrKW Macro research.

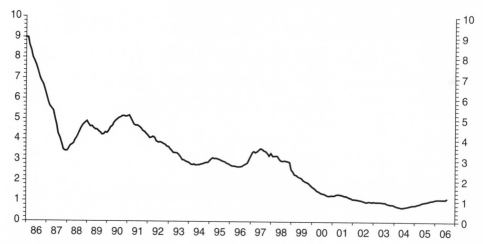

Figure 4.5 Average holding period for a stock on the LSE (years)
Source: DrKW Macro research.

However, long time horizons don't come naturally to us humans. When we are faced with the possibility of a reward, our brains release dopamine. Dopamine makes people feel good about themselves, confident and stimulated. The majority of dopamine receptors are located in areas of the brain that are generally associated with the X-system (our fast and dirty mental system). The possibility of monetary reward seems to trigger the release of dopamine in the same way as enjoying food, or taking pleasure-inducing drugs (see Knutson and Peterson, 2005).

McClure *et al.* (2004) have recently investigated the neural systems that underlie decisions surrounding delayed gratification. Much research has suggested that people tend to behave impatiently today but plan to act patiently in the future. For instance, when offered a choice between $10 today and $11 tomorrow, many people choose the immediate option. However, if you asked people today to choose between $10 in a year, and $11 in a year and a day, many of those who went for the immediate option in the first case now go for the second option.

In order to see what happens in the brain when faced with such choices, McClure *et al.* measured the brain activity of participants as they made a series of intertemporal choices between early and delayed monetary rewards. Some of the choice pairs included an immediate option; others were choices between two delayed options.

They found that when the choice involved an immediate gain, the ventral stratum (part of the basal ganglia), the medial orbitofrontal cortex, and the medial prefrontal cortex were all disproportionally used. All these elements are associated with the X-system. McClure *et al.* point out that these areas are also riddled by the mid-brain dopamine system. They note, 'These structures have consistently been implicated in impulsive behavior.'

When the choice involved two delayed rewards, the prefrontal and parietal cortex were engaged (correlates of the C-system). The more difficult the choice, the more these areas

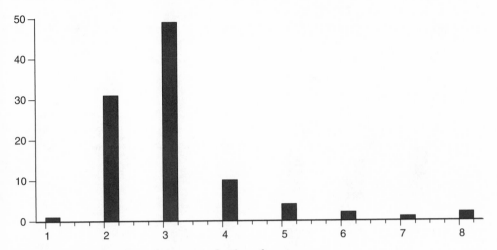

Figure 4.6 Frequency of cumulative years of underperformance
Source: DrKW Macro research.

seemed to be used. It is very hard for us to override the X-system. Frequently, the X-system reacts before the C-system has even had a chance to consider the problem. All too often, it looks as if we are likely to end up being hard-wired for the short term. So perhaps Keynes was right when he wrote, 'Investment based on genuine long-term expectation is so difficult today as to be scarcely practicable'. Patience really is a virtue.

In investment, loss aversion and time horizon are not independent issues. The more frequently you check a portfolio, the more likely it is that you will witness a loss. It is perfectly possible for a skilled fund manager to display three years of back-to-back declines. Figure 4.6 uses a constructed universe where all the fund managers have 3% alpha and a 6% tracking error. I then let the make-believe managers run money for 50 years. The chart illustrates the frequency of years of back-to-back underperformance. Around 70% of the make-believe fund managers displayed three or more years of underperformance!

A study by Goyal and Wahal (2005) shows why we need to explain the risks of investing to the end client far better than we currently do (Figure 4.7). It should be required reading by all pension plans and trustees. They review some 4000-plus decisions regarding the hiring and firing of investment manager by pension plan sponsors and trustees between 1993 and 2003. The results they uncover show the classic hallmarks of returns-chasing behavior. The funds the sponsors tend to hire have an average outperformance of nearly 14% in the three years before hiring, but they have statistically insignificant returns after the hiring. In contrast, those fired for performance reasons tend to have underperformed by around 6% in the three years leading up to the dismissal. However, in the three years after the firing, they tend to outperform by nearly 5%. A powerful lesson in the need to extend time horizons.

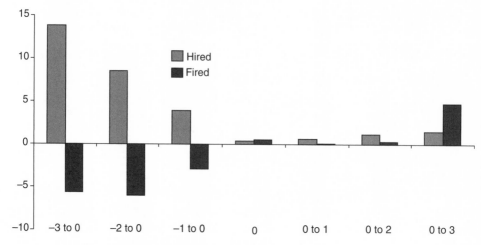

Figure 4.7 Performance around hiring and firing decisions (%)
Source: Goyal and Wahal (2005). DrKW Macro research.

SOCIAL PAIN AND THE HERDING HABIT

In the past, we have mentioned that there is strong evidence from neuroscience to suggest that real pain and social pain are felt in exactly the same places in the brain. Eisenberger and Lieberman (2004) asked participants to play a computer game. Players thought they were playing in a three-way game with two other players, throwing a ball back and forth.

In fact, the two other players were computer controlled. After a period of three-way play, the two other 'players' began to exclude the participant by throwing the ball back and forth between themselves. This social exclusion generates brain activity in the anterior cingulate cortex and the insula. Both of which are also activated by real physical pain.

Contrarian strategies are the investment equivalent of seeking out social pain. In order to implement such a strategy, you will buy the things that everyone else is selling, and sell the stocks that everyone else is buying. This is social pain. Eisenberger and Lieberman's results suggest that following such a strategy is like having your arm broken on a regular basis — not fun!

> To buy when others are despondently selling and sell when others are greedily buying requires the greatest fortitude and pays the greatest reward.
>
> Sir John Templeton

> It is the long-term investor, he who most promotes the public interest, who will in practice come in for the most criticism . . . For it is in the essence of his behavior that he should be eccentric, unconventional and rash in the eyes of average opinion.
>
> John Maynard Keynes

Worldly wisdom teaches that it is better for reputation to fail conventionally than to succeed unconventionally.

John Maynard Keynes

POOR STORIES

When a value screen is performed (or any other screen for that matter), a list of stocks is generated. Upon production of this list, the first thing everyone does is look down the list and start to analyze the elements. For instance, 'I can't buy that stock, it's a basket case'. The preconceived stories associated with stocks begin to interfere. Just as glamour stocks have seductive stories of incredible future growth, so value stocks have myriad reasons for their cheapness. All of which conspire to prevent the investor from actually following the screen's suggestions. So perhaps ignorance really is bliss in this context.

Stories are powerful because they trigger availability. Our minds are not limitless supercomputers; they are bounded by cognitive resource constraints. Very often people think of memory as functioning like a picture postcard or a photo. Unfortunately, this isn't the way memory works. Memory is a process, into which the truth is but one input. For instance, if you ask people, 'Which is a more likely cause of death in the US, shark attacks or lightning strikes?', a bizarrely large number of people seem to think that shark attacks are more common, despite the fact that 30 times more people are killed each year by lightning strikes than by shark attacks. The reason for this error in people's reasoning is that shark attacks are salient (easy to recall — largely thanks to *Jaws*) and available (every time someone gets nibbled off the coast of Florida or Hawaii, we all hear about it).

The same thing happens when we hear other stories. For instance, when an IPO is launched you can bet it will have a great story attached, full of the promise of growth. This makes the 'growth' salient and available, and all too often these thoughts then crowd out other considerations such as the valuation — just as the vivid shark attack crowds out the more likely lightning strike.

The reverse happens with value stocks. The stocks will generally appear to be cheap, but investors will be able to find any number of arguments as to why they are likely to stay cheap. So the story will crowd out the fact of cheapness.

OVERCONFIDENCE

One of the key reasons that people don't follow quant models is their amazing overconfidence in their own abilities. The same is true when it comes to value investing. Rather than follow a simple rule like, say, buying the bottom 20% of the MSCI universe ranked by PE, investors often prefer to rely on their stock selection skills (however dubious these may be).

Both the illusion of control and the illusion of knowledge conspire to generate this overconfidence. The illusion of knowledge fosters the idea that because we know more, we must be able to make superior decisions. Intuitively, it is easy to see why having more information should enable you to make better decisions. However, much evidence has been collected to show flaws in this idea. The empirical reality appears to be that more information isn't the same as better information. All too often investors suffer a signal extraction problem, that is to say they struggle to extract the meaningful elements among the deluge of noise.

The illusion of control also plays a part. We are experts in magical thinking — that is, believing we can influence things that we clearly can't. An article by Pronin *et al.* (2006) explores several aspects of this behavior. In one of their experiments, they told people they were investigating voodoo. Participants were paired (one of each pair actually worked for the experimenter and was either a pleasant person or a real pain in the neck). The stooge was always selected to be the 'victim', while the real participant was selected to stick pins into a voodoo doll ('witch doctor').

However, before they were asked to do this, they spent a little time with their partner in the experiment (who, remember, is either pleasant or exceedingly irritating). Then the 'witch doctor' was told to go into a room and generate 'vivid and concrete thoughts about the victim but not to say them aloud'. Then they were allowed to stick pins into a voodoo doll. After this, the experimenter asked the 'victim' if he had suffered any pains. Because he was a confederate of the experimenter he said 'yes, I have a bit of a headache'. The participant playing the witch doctor was then asked to complete a questionnaire including a question on the degree of culpability they felt for the 'victim's' pain. Amazingly, when dealing with the annoying 'victim', the 'witch doctors' felt much more responsible than they did with the normal 'victim', presumably because they had done more visualization of being angry at this person.

Several follow-up experiments were also conducted. One involved watching someone who was blindfolded throw a basketball. Participants were asked to either imagine the player making the shot, or imagine the player doing something else, like stretching. Those primed to think about the player making the shot thought they were much more responsible for the success or failure than those given the alternative scenario.

Finally, at a real basketball match, attendees were asked either to state how important a potential player was and why, or simply asked to describe the physical appearance of the player. After the match they were then asked to rate how responsible they felt for their team's performance. Once again, those primed to describe the players' importance felt much more responsible than those simply asked to describe the players (Figure 4.8).

In all three cases, those primed to think about the issues displayed significantly more 'magical thinking' than the controls. Investors are certainly likely to have thought about the stocks they are selecting, and as such will feel 'responsible' for the outcomes even if they can't possibly influence them.

FUN

The final stumbling block which I want to cover here is, simply, fun. As Keynes opined, 'The game of professional investment is intolerably boring and over-exacting to anyone who is

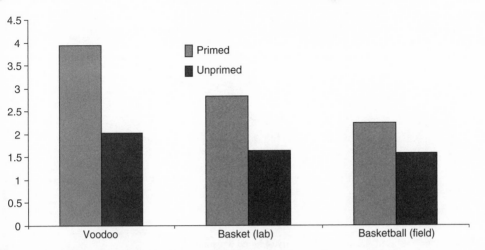

Figure 4.8 Degree of responsibility (1 = not responsible at all, 7 = totally responsible)
Source: Pronin *et al.* (2006). DrKW Macro research.

entirely exempt from the gambling instinct; while he who has it must pay this propensity the appropriate toll.'

Following simple rules and procedures isn't exactly great fun. Whereas filling your day by meeting companies and talking with sell-side analysts may be (although, personally, if this is your definition of fun, I suspect you need more help than I can offer you).

As Paul Samuelson said, 'Investing should be dull. It shouldn't be exciting. Investing should be more like watching paint dry or watching grass grow. If you want excitement, take $800 and go to Las Vegas.'

NO, HONESTLY I WILL BE GOOD

Let me end with one final word of warning: we all start out with the best of intentions but, as the saying goes, the road to hell is paved with good intentions. A recent paper by Koehler and Poon (2006) demonstrates the point perfectly. They asked participants to complete a questionnaire about giving blood at an upcoming donation clinic. People were asked to rate how likely they were to give blood, and also rate on a scale of 1 (strongly disagree) to 9 (strong agree) a series of statements concerning their attitudes on the subject, including a final question which read, 'Right now, as I think about it, I strongly intend to donate blood at the July 14–22 blood donation clinic.' This was used to gauge participants' current intention strength.

Figure 4.9 shows the predicted probability of blood donation and actual outcome of blood donation by the strength of current intentions. In general, people were massively too optimistic about their blood donation. On average, they were around 30 percentage points too optimistic. The predicted probability of blood donation rose much faster across the strength of current intentions than the actual outcome. This implies that current intentions have an overly strong effect on prediction of behavior, but not on behavior itself.

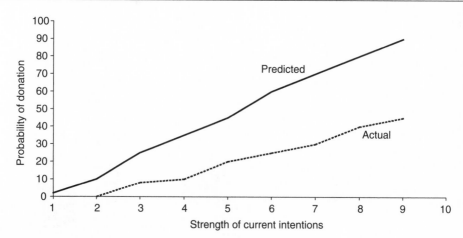

Figure 4.9   Predicted and actual probability of blood donation
Source: Koehler and Poon (2006). DrKW Macro research.

So as easy as it might be to say, 'From now on I'm going to be a value investor', the likelihood of it actually occurring is highly remote.

5
Placebos, Booze and Glamour Stocks[1]

Have you ever bought a (cheap) non-brand painkiller, and sworn that it didn't work as well as the (expensive) branded version? If so, your brain is probably playing tricks on you. We seem to have an in-built subconscious dislike of items that are at a discount. It is often said that in stock markets nobody likes a sale. Could a bias against cheapness be one of the causes of the value premium? The good news is that rational reflection seems to ameliorate this particular bias. The bad news is that staying rational while everyone else is losing their head is as hard as ever.

- It appears we are preprogrammed to equate price and quality. Now, in many contexts this may well be a useful heuristic. However, like most mental short cuts it can lead us far astray from rational decision making.
- For instance, which will work better: a painkiller that costs $2.50 per dose, or the same painkiller discounted and selling at just 10 cents? Rationally, they should have exactly the same effect (especially since both pills are nothing more than sugar pills). However, Dan Ariely and colleagues have found that people report the expensive version to be far more effective than the cheap version!
- If you prefer booze to pills, then consider the following. You are given some wine to taste and told it costs $10 a bottle, and then some more wine to taste and told it costs $90. The $90 wine was rated nearly twice as nice as the $10 wine. The only snag was that the wine was exactly the same in both cases. So we seem to display a bias against cheap goods.
- Could something similar be at work in the stock market? It is possible that investors tend to use the price = quality heuristic when considering stocks. It is often said that no one likes a sale in the stock market. Evidence from a new study by Statman *et al.* shows that the stocks that are most 'admired' tend to be those that have done well in both market and financial terms, and are relatively expensive. Those that are the most 'despised' tend to be poor past performers, and relatively cheap.
- Guess which wins out going forward? Strangely enough it is the most despised stocks that perform better in the future. Even after controlling for the market size, style and momentum, the despised stocks still generate an alpha of around 2% per annum.

---

[1]This article appeared in *Mind Matters* on 10 March 2008. Copyright © 2008 by The Société Générale Group. All rights reserved. The material discussed was accurate at the time of publication.

- What can be done to mitigate this bias against cheapness? The good news is that it appears that rational reflection can defeat the obsession with expense. So getting people to think carefully about the relationship between price and quality makes them more robust against this mental error. However, keeping a rational head on your shoulders when everyone else is losing theirs is likely to remain as hard as ever!

Have you ever bought a non-brand painkiller, taken it, and then thought it just wasn't as effective as the branded equivalent? If so the likelihood is that the brain is playing tricks on you. One of the everyday heuristics we seem to deploy is that price serves as a proxy for quality (much as confidence is used as a proxy for skill). Now, in many cases the price = quality heuristic works pretty well. For instance, buying an expensive pair of designer jeans will probably ensure a better fit and better quality workmanship than a pair bought at Walmart. However, this is not the case in every situation.

PAINKILLERS, PLACEBOS AND PRICE

Dan Ariely[2] and his colleagues have recently published a set of studies which cast some light upon the way we make decisions. The first study I wish to highlight was published in 2008 (Waber *et al.* 2008) and concerns the impact of price upon the perceived effectiveness of painkillers.

Ariely *et al.* subjected participants to electric shocks (what is it about psychologists and the desire to shock people — literally) in order to trigger pain. At first the shocks were mild, producing a tingling sensation. As the experiment progressed so the intensity of the shock increased. The final shock was enough to set your heart racing, and force your eyes wide open.

Before the shocks are administered you read a short brochure on the painkiller (Veladone-Rx) you will be testing. The information states that 'Veladone is an exciting new medication in the opioid family', and that 'Clinical studies show that over 92% of patients receiving Veladone in double-blind controlled studies reported significant pain relief within only 10 minutes, and that the pain relief lasted up to eight hours'. The literature also stated the price of the new drug. Some people received a price of $2.50 for a single dose; others saw a brochure that showed a discounted price of just 10 cents per dose.

After the first set of shocks was completed, subjects were given a cup of water and a pill — which they were told was Veladone. In fact it was a sugar pill. Fifteen minutes after taking the pill, they were subjected to the set of shocks once again, and asked whether the painkiller was effective or not.

The results that Ariely *et al.* uncovered are shown in Figure 5.1. When the subjects were told that Veladone cost $2.50, some 85% of them reported that they felt less pain after taking the drug. In contrast, when they thought Veladone cost only 10 cents, only 61% said that the painkiller was effective.

So Ariely and colleagues clearly show a placebo effect, because the pills given were nothing other than sugar pills. However, they also show that the price had a distinct impact upon this placebo effect; the higher the price, the more subjects felt it had worked.

This work has some radical implications for health care, obviously. Modern science has long demonstrated strong support for the impact of placebo treatments. In some ways doctors

---

[2]Dan has made a disproportionate number of appearances in my notes as he is one of the keenest observers of human nature I have come across. In addition, his research topics are always fascinating. He has recently written a book *Predictably Irrational*, which I suggest that everyone reads. It will certainly make my next reading list review. Personally I think *Predictably Irrational* will be the *Freakanomics* of the behavioral psychological world.

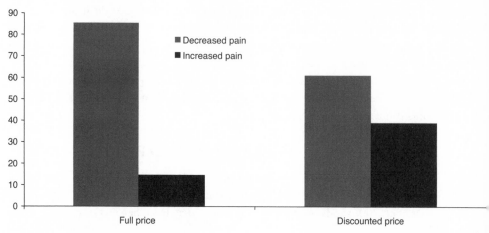

Figure 5.1   Percentage of subjects reporting
Source: Waber *et al.* (2008).

have been exploiting placebo effects for years. For instance, often when you go to the doctor with a sore throat, he or she will give you antibiotics. However, somewhere around one-third of sore throats are caused by viruses — upon which antibiotics have absolutely no effect. Instead we all end up taking too many antibiotics and help to create drug-resistant bacterial infections which threaten us all. Perhaps doctors should just prescribe an expensive sugar pill rather than antibiotics the next time they come across a viral infection.

DOES EXPENSIVE WINE TASTE BETTER?

The next example comes from a great study by Plassmann *et al.* (2008). They gave subjects five wines to taste, and asked them to rate each of the wines. All the wines were Cabernet Sauvignons. In fact, only three different wines were used in the experiment, as two wines were presented twice. In the first version of the experiment subjects were told the price of each wine. For example, Wine 2 was presented once as $90, and once as $10 (Table 5.1).

Table 5.1   Which wine in which bottle?

Stated cost	Real wine
$5 wine	Wine 1
$10 wine	Wine 2
$35 wine	Wine 3
$45 wine	Wine 1
$90 wine	Wine 2

Source: Plassmann *et al.* (2008).

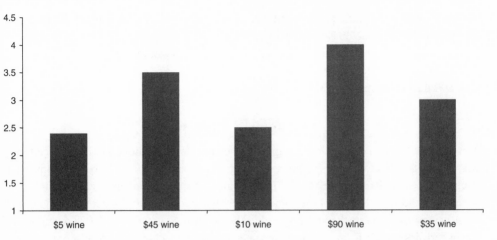

Figure 5.2   Average rating of the wine (1 = didn't like, 6 = really loved) with price information
Source: Plassmann *et al.* (2008).

Figure 5.2 shows the scores the subjects awarded the wines based on a scale of 1 (didn't like at all) to 6 (really loved it). When faced with Wine 2 in the guise of a $10 bottle the average rating was around 2.4. However, when told the same bottle was a $90 bottle the average rating jumped to 4. In fact, the bottle retailed at $90!

A similar finding is true of Wine 1. So effectively price tends to an increase in perceived taste ratings of between 50 and 60%!

To ensure that it was the price that was driving the result, Plassmann *et al.* repeated the test, this time without the price disclosed. The results are shown in Figure 5.3. When the

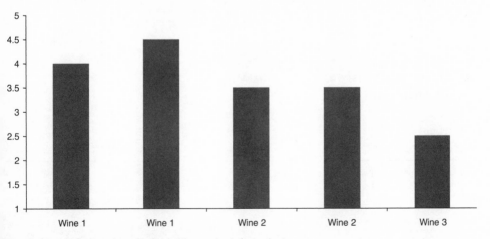

Figure 5.3   Average rating of wine (without price information)
Source: Plassmann *et al.* (2008).

price was absent the participants found that when presented with the same wine twice they rated the wine the same on each occasion.

The wines in the two charts are placed in comparable positions. This reveals that when told the wine was cheap (i.e. $5) people really marked the wine down, and when told a wine cost $90 they massively increased its ratings!

GLAMOUR STOCKS

Is it possible that something similar happens when people think about investing? It certainly seems plausible that investors might think that an expensive stock is a better option than a cheap stock as its expense might signal quality — just as people seem to think with painkillers and wine. Are stocks just another item that people dislike when they are on sale?

A new paper suggests that this may indeed be the case. Statman *et al.* (2008) examine the characteristics and performance of stocks rated as the most admired or despised in terms of their long-term investment value in the *Fortune* magazine's annual survey of companies. The period they study covers 1982–2006.

Table 5.2 shows the key characteristics of the stocks in each of the portfolios. The stocks in the admired portfolio are certainly 'better' firms. They have an average sales growth of 10% per annum over the last two years, compared with the 3.5% growth achieved by the despised stocks. They have done noticeably better over both the immediate past and the medium term (as measured by momentum). The admired stocks also tend to be more expensive, showing an average P/CF ratio of 9.7× vs 7.3× for the despised stocks.[3]

Table 5.2 Characteristics of admired and despised companies

Characteristic	Admired companies	Despised companies
P/E	15.0	12.6
P/B	2.0	1.3
P/CF	9.7	7.3
Sales growth (last 2 years)	10.0%	3.5%
Earnings growth (last 2 years)	12.7%	5.2%
ROA	15.8%	12.5%
12M returns	21.5%	11.0%
36M returns	81.2%	38.4%

Source: Statman *et al.* (2008).

---

[3]A similar pattern can be found among analyst recommendations. See Chapter 10 of *Behavioural Investing* for more details.

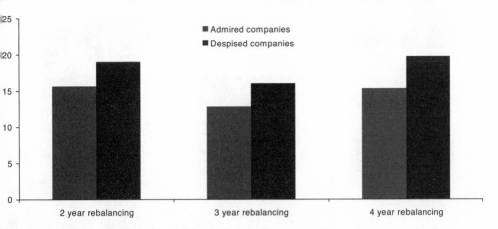

Figure 5.4 Performance of admired and despised stocks (% per annum)
Source: Statman *et al.* (2008).

However, Statman *et al.* then monitor the performance of stocks over time, and Figure 5.4 shows the results they uncover. The despised stocks do significantly better than the admired stocks. This result holds even when returns are adjusted for market, size, style and momentum! For instance, with a four-year rebalancing, the despised stocks have a four-factor alpha of just over 2% per annum and the admired stocks have a marginally negative alpha.

BEATING THE BIAS

The good news is that it appears that cognitive reflection (that is, simply thinking about it) helps to counteract the 'automatic' equating of price and quality. In order to illustrate this we turn to the work of Shi *et al.* (2005). They explore the impact of a 'mental energy' drink upon people's ability to solve anagrams. Before the drink was distributed participants were told that they would be charged for the cost of the drink. Some were told they would pay the full price ($1.89), others were told the full price was normally $1.89, but the university had used a bulk order to reduce the cost to $0.89.

Figure 5.5 shows the results that Shiv *et al.* discovered. The control group just solved anagrams without the aid of the drink. However, note the marked deterioration in the performance of those who received a discounted drink! They solved around three less puzzles than the control group or the full price group. So Shiv *et al.* find strong evidence of a negative placebo effect (the discounting hurt performance) but the full price drink didn't increase performance!

In a second experiment, Shiv *et al.* drew attention to the price–efficacy link by asking participants to rate the the drink after reading the following two statements. 'Given the price I was charged for SoBe (the name of the drink), I feel that SoBe is "very bad" (a rating of 1)/"very good" (7) at improving mental performance'; and 'Given the price I was charged for SoBe, I feel that SoBe is "very bad" (1)/"very good" (7) at improving concentration'.

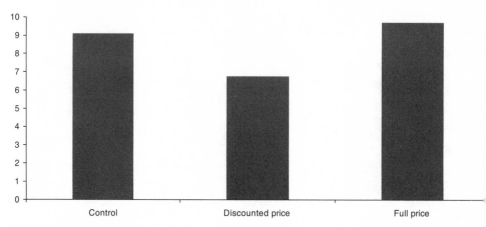

Figure 5.5 Number of puzzles solved
Source: Shiv *et al.* (2008).

The results are shown in Figure 5.6. There is no difference in the number of puzzles solved regardless of the price charged for the drink. So simply directing people to think about the link (or lack thereof) between price and quality seems to ameliorate the effect. This also suggests that the link between price and quality is generally a function of some subconscious mental process.

Could it be that value investors have learned to override their 'natural' subconscious price = quality heuristic? After all, most value investors tend to spend a very long time analyzing intrinsic value, effectively reflecting the use of rational tools rather than gut feelings.

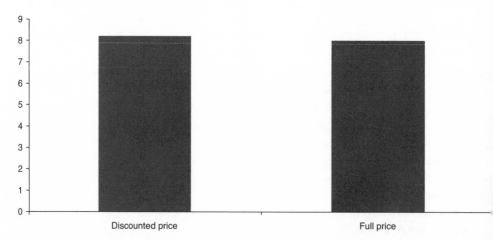

Figure 5.6 Number of puzzles solved
Source: Shiv *et al.* (2005).

6

Keep It Simple, Stupid[1]

Too much time is spent trying to find out more and more about less and less, until we know everything about nothing. Rarely, if ever, do we stop and ask what we actually need to know!

- Our industry is obsessed with the minutia of detail. Analysts are often petrified of saying 'I don't know'. Something I personally have never had any issue with! It is a common misunderstanding that in order to make good decisions we need masses of information. However, nothing could be further from the truth.
- A new paper by Tsai *et al.* examines the confidence and accuracy of American football fans trying to predict the outcome of games. They found that people were just as accurate if they had six items of information as when they had 30! However, confidence (which exceeded accuracy at all levels of information) increased massively as the amount of information increased.
- This inability to process large amounts of information represents a cognitive constraint embedded within our brains. The simple truth is that our brains aren't supercomputers with limitless computational power. Rather than crashing mindlessly into our cognitive bounds, we should seek to exploit our natural endowment. So, rather than collecting endless amounts of information, we should spend more time working out what is actually important, and focusing upon that.
- When it comes to information overload, parallels exist between medicine and investing. For instance, in a certain hospital in Michigan, doctors were sending around 90% of all patients with severe chest pains to the cardiac care unit. However, they were admitting 90% of those who needed to be admitted, and 90% of those who didn't! They were doing no better than chance.
- The key reason for this seems to have been that the doctors were looking at the wrong information — effectively they were looking at a wide range of 'risk' factors such as age, gender, weight, smoking, etc. While these factors can define our probability of having a heart attack, they aren't good diagnostic tools to tell if you are actually having a heart attack.

- A complex set of statistical tables were introduced to help doctors make better decisions. However, when these were removed, the doctors still made good decisions. They had learned to look at the correct information cues to make the best decision. Doctors using very simple decision tree diagram delivered the best results. Similar devices could easily be deployed in the world of investing. As Warren Buffett says, 'investing is simple but not easy'.

At the start of the year I did a two-hour Q&A session with a client on behavioral decision making. At the end of the session, my host walked me out and said, 'If you had to pick one word to describe your message which one would you choose?' My response was 'simplify'.

I have written before about the illusion of knowledge,[2] and when I present, I spend a reasonable amount of time talking about our obsession with knowing more and more about less and less, until we end up knowing nothing about everything. But rarely if ever do we stop and ask what do I need to know in order to actually take an investment decision.

In the past I have often used the work of Paul Slovic to illustrate that more information isn't necessarily better information. However, Slovic's work was published in 1973, and in the interests of replication and robustness I'm delighted to say that three researchers have recently shown exactly the same patterns that were uncovered by Slovic.

IS MORE BETTER?

Tsai, *et al.* (2008) show once again that, beyond a remarkably low level, more information translates into excessive confidence and static accuracy. They tested American football fans' ability to predict the outcome and point spread in 15 NCAA games. The information (selected by surveying non-participating football fans) was presented in a random order over five rounds. Each round revealed six items of information (called cues).

The information provided deliberately excluded team names as these were too leading. Instead they covered a wide range of statistics on football such as own fumbles, turnover margin, and yards gained.

Participants were 30 college and graduate students at the University of Chicago. On average, participants spent about one hour to complete the experiment in exchange for a fixed payment of $15. In addition, a reward of $50 was promised to the participant with the best performance. In order to take part in the study, participants had to pass a test demonstrating that they were highly knowledgeable about college football.

To see if more information was better information from a benchmark point of view, a stepwise logic regression was run on games not used in the actual test. While this sounds incredibly complex, all it really means is that new information was made available to the computer model in each round. This replicates the conditions faced by the experiment's human participants.

The results are shown in Figure 6.1. With just the first set of information (six cues) the model was around 56% accurate. As information was gradually added, the predictive accuracy rose up to 71% by the time all the available information was presented.

---

[2] See Chapters 2 and 11 of *Behavioural Investing* (Wiley, 2007).

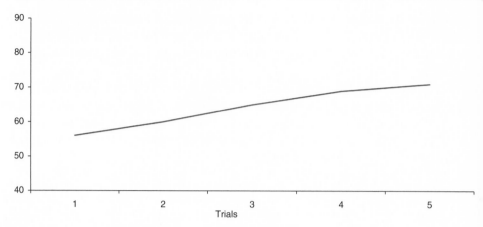

Figure 6.1   Accuracy of prediction from the computer model (%)
Source: Tsai *et al.* (2007).

So, from a statistical modeling point of view, more information was indeed better information. However, when dealing with humans rather than computers a very different result was uncovered. The average performance of the participants is shown in Figure 6.2. Accuracy pretty much flatlines at around 62% regardless of the amount of information that was being provided. This performance is higher than the model on the earlier rounds, although not statistically so, but lower in the later rounds.

However, confidence tends to soar as more information is added. So, it starts off at 69% with 6 cues, and rises to nearly 80% by the time participants have 30 cues. So, just as with Slovic's original study, confidence but not accuracy increases with the amount of information available.

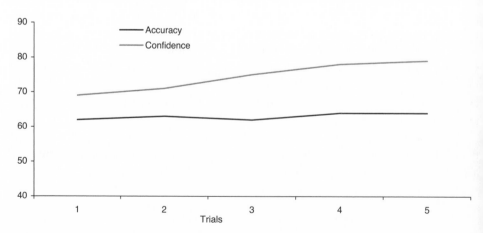

Figure 6.2   Accuracy and confidence of predictions from participants
Source: Tsai *et al.* (2007).

This finding reflects the cognitive constraints suffered by the human mind. As George Miller found in 1956, the average human working memory (the brain's scratch pad, if you like) can handle seven bits of information (plus or minus 2).

Long before George Miller had discovered this cognitive bound, none other than Sir Arthur Conan Doyle had written the following words uttered by the ever insightful Sherlock Holmes:

> I consider that a man's brain originally is like a little empty attic, and you have to stock it with such furniture as you choose. A fool takes in all the lumber of every sort that he comes across, so that the knowledge which might be useful to him gets crowded out, or at best is jumbled up with a lot of other things, so that he has a difficulty laying his hands upon it. But the skillful workman is very careful indeed as to what he takes into his brain-attic. He will have nothing but the tools which may help him in doing his work, but of these he has a large assortment, and all in the most perfect order. It is a mistake to think that the little room has elastic walls and can distend to any extent. Depend upon it, there comes a time when for every addition of knowledge you forget something you knew before. It is of the highest importance, therefore, not to have useless facts elbowing out the useful ones.

A Study in Scarlet

The simple truth is that we aren't supercomputers with unlimited power. Rather than trying to push the cognitive bounds of our brains, we should seek to best exploit our natural endowment. So, rather than collecting all the available information, we should spend more time working out what is actually important and focus on that.

KISS: KEEP IT SIMPLE, STUPID

Yet more evidence of our limited mental capacity is provided by a recent study by Dijksterhuis *et al.* (2006). In their study participants were asked to choose among 4 different cars. They faced one of two conditions: they were either given just four attributes per car (low load) or 12 attributes per car (high load). In both cases, one of the cars was noticeably 'better' than the others, with some 75% of its attributes being positive. Two cars had 50% of the attributes positive, and one car had only 25% of the attributes positive.

Figure 6.3 shows the percentage of participants choosing the 'best' car under each of the information conditions. Under the low level of information condition nearly 60% of subjects chose the best car. However, when faced with information overload, only around 20% of subjects chose the best car!

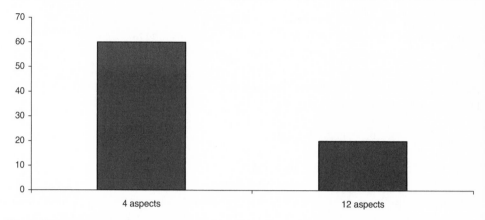

Figure 6.3   Percentage of participants choosing the 'best' car
Source: Dijksterhuis *et al.* (2007)

LESSONS FROM HEART ATTACKS

The original work in this field was done by Lee Green (Green and Yates, 1995). The problem arose in a hospital in Michigan. Physicians at this particular hospital tended to send around 90% of all patients with severe chest pains to the cardiac care unit. The unit was becoming seriously overcrowded, care standards were dropping and costs were rising.

The decision to send so many patients to ICU reflected concerns among doctors over the costs of a false negative (i.e. not admitting someone who should have been admitted). Fine, you might say, rather that than the alternative. However, this ignores the risks inherent in entering ICU. Around 20,000 Americans die every year from a hospital transmitted illness. The risks of contracting such a disease are markedly higher in ICU than in a conventional ward.

The most damning problem for the Michigan hospital doctors was that they sent around 90% of those who needed to be admitted and around 90% of those who didn't need to be admitted to ICU. They did no better than chance!

WHY?

Such a performance begs the question of why doctors found it so difficult to separate out those who needed specialist care from those who didn't. Green and Yates sought to explore exactly this issue.

The bottom line from their research was that doctors were looking at the wrong things. They tended to overweight 'risk factors' such as a family history of premature coronary artery disease, age, male gender, smoking, diabetes mellitus, increased serum cholesterol, and hypertension.

However, while these factors help to assess the overall likelihood of someone having cardiac ischemia, they have little diagnostic power. They aren't effective information cues, or as Green and Yates label them, they are pseudodiagnostic items. That is to say, 'they are additional information related to the diagnosis under consideration that influences decision makers' probability judgements but that are not of objective value in making the distinction between that diagnosis and other possibilities'.

Much better diagnostic cues are available. Research has revealed that the nature and location of patients' symptoms, their history of ischemic disease, and certain specific electrocardiographic findings are by far the most powerful predictors of acute ischemia, infarction, and mortality.

CAN ANYTHING BE DONE?

Green and his colleagues came up with the idea of using laminated cards with various probabilities marked against diagnostic information. The doctors could then follow these tables and multiply the probabilities according to the symptoms and test findings in order to estimate the overall likelihood of a problem. If this was above a set threshold then the patient was to be admitted to cardiac ICU, otherwise a normal bed with a monitor would suffice.

After this aid to decision making was introduced, there was a marked improvement in the decision making of the doctors. They still caught a high proportion of problem cases, but they cut down dramatically on sending patients to ICU who didn't need to go.

Of course, this might indicate that the tool had worked. But, being good and conscientious scientists, Green et al. decided they had better check to ensure that this was the case. This was done by giving the doctors the decision making tool in some weeks, and not giving them in other weeks. Obviously, if the tool is the source of the improved performance one would expect some deterioration in performance in the weeks when access to the aid was prohibited.

The results from this experiment showed something surprising. Decision making seemed to have improved regardless of the use of the tool! What could account for this surprising finding? Was it possible that doctors had memorized the probabilities from the cards, and were using them even when the cards weren't available?

This seemed unlikely as the various combinations and permutations listed on the card were not easy to recall. A quick test showed something else was afoot. In fact, the doctors had managed to assimilate the correct cues. That is to say, by showing them the correct items to use for diagnosis, the doctors emphasis switched from pseudodiagnostic information to truly informative elements. They started looking at the right things!

SIMPLICITY IS KEY

Based on this experience Green and Mehr (1997) designed a very easy-to-use decision aid, a series of yes/no questions (several orders of magnitude easier than the probability based measures originally built). The structure of the aid is shown in Figure 6.4.

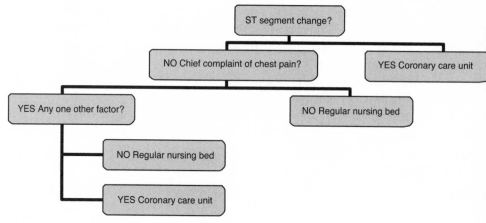

Figure 6.4   Admission decision for suspected MI
Source: Green and Mehr (1997).

If the patient displays a particular electrocardiogram anomaly (the ST change) then he is admitted to ICU straight away. If not, then a second cue is considered: whether the patient is suffering chest pains. If he is, then again he is admitted to ICU, and so forth.

This makes the critical elements of the decision transparent and salient to the doctor. It also works exceptionally well in practice. Figure 6.5 shows the accuracy of the measures we have discussed here. The axes represent the two dimensions of our problem, the proportion of heart attack patients who are correctly diagnosed and sent to the ICU (vertical axis) and the proportion of non-heart attack patients who are also sent to ICU (horizontal axis).

The 45 degree line represents pure chance. Points above the diagonal represent a performance better than chance, while below the diagonal represents a worse than luck outcome.

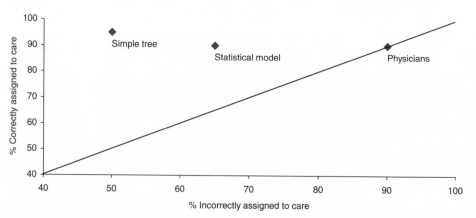

Figure 6.5   Performance of various groups in MI diagnosis
Source: Gigerenzer (2007).

The doctors originally did slightly worse than chance (as discussed). The complex probability model can be set for various trade-offs, but I've selected the optimum trade-off to ensure that the highest proportion of those with heart attacks are correctly diagnosed. It is a marked improvement on the doctors' solo efforts; it characterizes more heart attack patients correctly, and vastly reduces the number of needless ICU admissions.

However, the simple decision tree does even better. It offers an even higher correct diagnosis and even greater reduction in needless admissions! So, fast and frugal decision making pays off in this domain.

EXPERTS FOCUS ON THE KEY INFORMATION

It is also noteworthy that Reyna and Lloyd (2006) explored heart attack diagnosis among various levels of experts. They found that the higher the level of expertise, the less information they needed to make accurate decisions. The experts essentially focused simply on what mattered most, and didn't allow themselves to be distracted by extraneous information.

Figure 6.6 highlights the correlations across knowledge groups between the myocardial infarction (heart attack) (MI) risk and the coronary artery disease (CAD) probability. The medical students decisions on admission were heavily influenced by both CAD and MI risks. In fact this pattern held until one got to the level of cardiologists. The highest skilled group, the cardiology experts only looked at the MI risks. Again this finding highlights the power of thinking about what matters rather than obsessing with ever more information.

FROM THE EMERGENCY ROOM TO THE MARKETS

Back to investment. Could something similar be designed for investors? Richard Thaler (one of the founding fathers of the field of behavioral finance) has recently referred to this kind

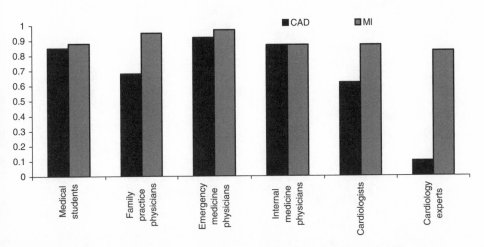

Figure 6.6   Correlations between MI risk and CAD probability with admission probability
Source: Reyna and Lloyd (2006).

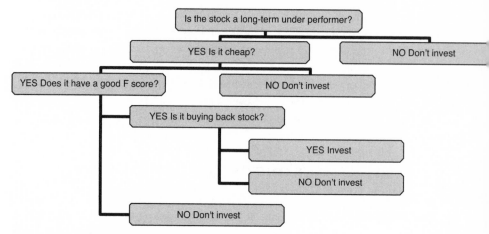

Figure 6.7   A simple contrarian decision tree
Source: SG Global Strategy research.

of work as choice architecture. The essential aim is to help people make good decisions by using rebiasing rather than debiasing. I have regularly urged investors to think about the factors that really matter for investment, one could easily imagine a fast and frugal decision making tree like the one shown in Figure 6.7 to help keep investors focused on what really matters.

Investors may be well advised to remember the sage words of Warren Buffett 'Investing is simple but not easy'!

Six Impossible Things before Breakfast, or, How EMH Has Damaged Our Industry[1]

The efficient markets hypothesis (EMH) is the financial equivalent of Monty Python's Dead Parrot. No matter how much you point out that it is dead, the believers just respond that it is simply resting! I wouldn't really care if EMH was just some academic artefact, but as Keynes noted, 'practical men are usually the slaves of some defunct economist'. The EMH has left us with a litany of bad ideas, from CAPM to benchmarking, and risk management to shareholder value. The worst of its legacy is the terrible advice it offers on how to outperform — essentially be a better forecaster than everyone else. It is surely time to consign both the EMH and its offshoots to the dustbin of history.

- Academic theories have a very high degree of path dependence. Once a theory has been accepted it seems to take forever to dislodge it. As Max Planck said, 'Science advances one funeral at a time'. The EMH debate takes on almost religious tones on occasions. At one conference, Gene Fama yelled 'God knows markets are efficient!' This sounds like a prime example of belief bias to me (a tendency to judge by faith rather than by evidence).
- The EMH bothers me less as an academic concept (albeit an irrelevant one) than it does as a source of hindrance to sensible investing. EMH has left us with a long list of bad ideas that have influenced our industry. For instance, the capital asset pricing model (CAPM) leads to the separation of alpha and beta, which ends up distracting from the real aim of investment — 'Maximum real total returns after tax' as Sir John Templeton put it.
- This approach has also given rise to the obsession with benchmarking, and indeed a new species, Homo Ovinus — whose only concern is where it stands relative to the rest of the crowd, the living embodiment of Keynes' edict, 'That it is better for reputation to fail conventionally, than succeed unconventionally'.
- The EMH also lies at the heart of risk management, option pricing theory, and the dividend and capital structure irrelevance theorems of Modigliani and Miller, and the concept of shareholder value, all of which have inflicted serious damage upon investors. However, the most insidious aspects of the EMH are the advice it offers as to the sources

---

[1]This article appeared in *Mind Matters* on 17 June 2009. Copyright © 2009 by The Société Générale Group. All rights reserved. The material discussed was accurate at the time of publication.

of outperformance. The first is inside information, which is, of course, illegal. The second is that to outperform you need to forecast the future better than everyone else. This has sent the investment industry on a wild goose chase for decades.

- The prima facie case against EMH is the existence of bubbles. The investment firm, GMO defines a bubble as at least a two-standard-deviation move from (real) trend. Under EMH, a two-standard-deviation event should occur roughly every 44 years. However, GMO found some 30-plus bubbles since 1925 — that is slightly more than one every three years!

- The supporters of EMH fall back on what they call their 'Nuclear Bomb', the failure of active management to outperform the index. However, this is to confuse the absence of evidence with the evidence of absence. Additionally, recent research shows that career risk minimization is the defining characteristic of institutional investment. They don't even try to outperform!

What follows is the text of a speech to be delivered at the CFA UK conference on 'Whatever happened to EMH?', dedicated to Peter Bernstein. Peter will be fondly remembered and sadly missed by all who work in investment. Although he and I often ended up on opposite sides of the debates, he was a true gentleman and always a pleasure to discuss ideas with. I am sure Peter would have disagreed with some, much and perhaps all of my speech, but I'm equally sure he would have enjoyed the discussion.

THE DEAD PARROT OF FINANCE

Given that this is the UK division of the CFA I am sure that The Monty Python Dead Parrot Sketch will be familiar to all of you. The EMH is the financial equivalent of the Dead Parrot (Figure 7.1). I feel like the John Cleese character (an exceedingly annoyed customer who recently purchased a parrot) returning to the petshop to berate the owner:

> E's passed on! This parrot is no more! He has ceased to be! 'E's expired and gone to meet 'is maker. 'E's a stiff! Bereft of life, 'E rests in peace! If you hadn't nailed 'im to the perch 'E'd be pushing up the daisies! 'Is metabolic processes are now 'istory! 'E's off the twig! 'E's kicked the bucket, 'E's shuffled off 'is mortal coil, run down the curtain and joined the bleedin' choir invisible!! This is an ex-parrot!!

The shopkeeper (picture Gene Fama if you will) keeps insisting that the parrot is simply resting. Incidentally, the Dead Parrot Sketch takes on even more meaning when you recall Stephen Ross's words that 'All it takes to turn a parrot into a learned financial economist is just one word — arbitrage'.

The EMH supporters have strong similarities with the Jesuit astronomers of the 17th century who desperately wanted to maintain the assumption that the Sun revolved around the Earth. The reason for this desire to protect the maintained hypothesis was simple. If the Sun didn't revolve around the Earth, then the Bible's tale of Joshua asking God to make the Sun stand still in the sky was a lie. A bible that lies even once can't be the inerrant foundation for faith!

Figure 7.1 The dead parrot of finance!
Source: SG Global Strategy research.

The efficient market hypothesis (EMH) has done massive amounts of damage to our industry. But before I explore some errors embedded within the approach and the havoc they have wreaked, I would like to say a few words on why the EMH exists at all.

Academic theories are notoriously subject to path dependence (or hysteresis, if you prefer). Once a theory has been adopted it takes an enormous amount of effort to dislocate it. As Max Planck said, 'Science advances one funeral at a time.'

The EMH has been around in one form or another since the Middle Ages (the earliest debate I can find is between St Thomas Aquinas and other monks on the 'just' price to charge for corn, with St Thomas arguing that the 'just' price was the market price). Just imagine we had all grown up in a parallel universe. David Hirschleifer did exactly that: welcome to his world of the Deficient Markets Hypothesis.

A school of sociologists at the University of Chicago is proposing the Deficient Markets Hypothesis — that prices inaccurately reflect all information. A brilliant Stanford psychologist, call him Bill Blunte, invents the Deranged Anticipation and Perception Model (DAPM), in which proxies for market misevaluation are used to predict security returns. Imagine the euphoria when researchers discovered that these mispricing proxies (such as book/market, earnings/price and past returns), and mood indicators (such as amount of sunlight) turned out to be strong predictors of future returns. At this point, it would seem that the Deficient Markets Hypothesis was the best-confirmed theory in social science.

To be sure, dissatisfied practitioners would have complained that it is harder to actually make money than the ivory tower theorists claim. One can even imagine some academic heretics documenting rapid short-term stock market responses to news arrival in event studies, and arguing that security return predictability results from rational premia for bearing risk. Would the old guard surrender easily? Not when they could appeal to intertemporal versions of the DAPM, in which mispricing is only corrected slowly. In such a setting, short window event studies cannot uncover the market's inefficient response to new information. More generally, given the strong theoretical underpinnings of market inefficiency, the rebels would have an uphill fight.

In finance we seem to have a chronic love affair with elegant theories. Our faculties for critical thinking seem to have been overcome by the seductive power of mathematical beauty. A long long time ago, when I was a young and impressionable lad starting out in my study of economics, I too was enthralled by the bewitching beauty and power of the EMH/rational expectations approach (akin to the Dark Side in Star Wars). However, in practice we should always remember that there are no points for elegance!

My own disillusionment with EMH and the ultra rational *Homo Economicus* that it rests upon came in my third year of university. I sat on the oversight committee for my degree course as a student representative. At the university I attended it was possible to elect to graduate with a specialism in Business Economics, if you took a prescribed set of courses. The courses necessary to attain this degree were spread over two years. It wasn't possible to do all the courses in one year, so students needed to stagger their electives. Yet at the beginning of the third year I was horrified to find students coming to me to complain that they hadn't realized this! These young economists had failed to solve the simplest two-period optimization problem I can imagine! What hope for the rest of the world? Perhaps I am living evidence that finance is like smoking. Ex-smokers always seem to provide the most ardent opposition to anyone lighting up. Perhaps the same thing is true in finance!

THE QUEEN OF HEARTS AND IMPOSSIBLE BELIEFS

I'm quite sure the Queen of Hearts would have made an excellent EMH economist.

> Alice laughed: 'There's no use trying,' she said; 'one can't believe impossible things.' I daresay you haven't had much practice,' said the Queen. 'When I was younger, I always did it for half an hour a day. Why, sometimes I've believed as many as six impossible things before breakfast.'

> *Lewis Carroll*, Alice in Wonderland.

Earlier I alluded to a startling lack of critical thinking in finance. This lack of 'logic' isn't specific to finance; in general we, as a species, suffer belief bias. There is a tendency to evaluate the validity of an argument on the basis of whether or not one agrees with the conclusion, rather than on whether or not it follows logically from the premise. Consider these four syllogisms:

1. No police dogs are vicious
   Some highly trained dogs are vicious
   Therefore some highly trained dogs are not police dogs

2. No nutritional things are inexpensive
   Some vitamin pills are inexpensive
   Therefore, some vitamin pills are not nutritional

3. No addictive things are inexpensive
   Some cigarettes are inexpensive
   Therefore, some addictive things are not cigarettes

4. No millionaires are hard workers
   Some rich people are hard workers
   Therefore, some millionaires are not rich people

These four syllogisms provide us with a mixture of validity and believability. Table 7.1 separates out the problems along these two dimensions. This enables us to assess which criteria people use in reaching their decisions.

Table 7.1   Validity and belief

		Belief	
		Believable	Unbelievable
Logic	Valid	Dogs (VB)	Vitamins (VU)
	Invalid	Cigarettes (IB)	Millionaires (IU)

Source: SG Equity Strategy.

As Figure 7.2 reveals, it is the believability not the validity of the concept that seems to drive behavior. When validity and believability coincide, then 90% of subjects reach the correct conclusion. However, when the puzzle is invalid but believable, some 66% still accepted the conclusion as true. When the puzzle is valid but unbelievable only around 60% of subjects accepted the conclusion as true. Thus we have a tendency to judge things by their believability rather than their validity — which is clear evidence that logic goes out of the window when beliefs are strong.

All this talk about beliefs makes EMH sound like a religion. Indeed, it has some overlap with religion in that belief appears to be based on faith rather than proof. Debating the subject can also give rise to the equivalent of religious fanaticism. In his book *The New Finance: The Case Against Efficient Markets,* Robert Haugen (long regarded as a heretic by many in finance) recalls a conference he was speaking at where he listed various inefficiencies. Gene Fama was in the audience and at one point yelled; 'You're a criminal . . . God knows markets are efficient.'

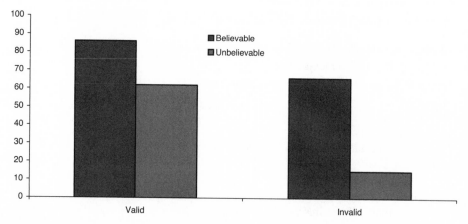

Figure 7.2   Percentage accepting conclusion as true
Source: Evans *et al.* (1983).

SLAVES OF SOME DEFUNCT ECONOMIST

To be honest I wouldn't really care if EMH was just some academic artefact. The real damage unleashed by the EMH stems from the fact that, as Keynes long ago noted, 'practical men . . . are usually the slaves of some defunct economist.'

So let's turn to the investment legacy with which the EMH has burdened us: first off is the capital asset pricing model (CAPM). I won't dwell on the flaws here, but suffice it to say that my view is that CAPM is CRAP (completely redundant asset pricing).

The aspects of CAPM that we do need to address here briefly are those that hinder the investment process — one of the most pronounced of which is the obsession with performance measurement. The separation of alpha and beta is at best an irrelevance and at worst a serious distraction from the true nature of investment. Sir John Templeton said it best when he observed that 'the aim of investment is maximum real returns after tax'. Yet instead of focusing on this target, we have spawned one industry that does nothing other than pigeon-hole investors into categories.

As the late, great Bob Kirby opined, 'Performance measurement is one of those basically good ideas that somehow got totally out of control. In many cases, the intense application of performance measurement techniques has actually served to impede the purpose it is supposed to serve.'

The obsession with benchmarking also gives rise to one of the biggest sources of bias in our industry — career risk. For a benchmarked investor, risk is measured as tracking error. This gives rise to Homo Ovinus (Figure 7.3) — a species who is concerned purely with where he stands relative to the rest of the crowd. (For those who aren't up in time to

Figure 7.3   Homo Ovinus
Source: Worth1000.com.

listen to Farming Today, Ovine is the proper name for sheep.) This species is the living embodiment of Keynes' edict that 'it is better for reputation to fail conventionally than to succeed unconventionally'. More on this poor creature a little later.

While on the subject of benchmarking we can't leave without observing that EMH and CAPM also give rise to market indexing. Only in an efficient market is a market cap-weighted index the 'best' index. If markets aren't efficient then cap weighting leads us to overweight the most expensive stocks and underweight the cheapest stocks!

Before we leave risk behind, we should also note the way in which fans of EMH protect themselves against evidence that anomalies such as value and momentum exist. In a wonderfully tautological move, they argue that only risk factors can generate returns in an efficient market, so these factors must clearly be risk factors!

Those of us working in the behavioral camp argue that behavioral and institutional biases are the root causes of the outperformance of the various anomalies. I have even written papers showing that value isn't riskier than growth on any definition that the EMH fans might choose to use.

For instance, if we take the simplest definition of risk used by the EMH fans (the standard deviation of returns), then Figure 7.4 shows an immediate issue for EMH. The return on value stocks is higher than the return on growth stocks, but the so-called 'risk' of value stocks is lower than the risk of growth stocks — in complete contradiction to the EMH viewpoint.

This overt focus on risk has again given rise to what is in my view yet another largely redundant industry — risk management. The tools and techniques are deeply flawed. The use of measures such as VaR give rise to the illusion of safety. All too often they use trailing inputs calculated over short periods of time, and forget that their model inputs are effectively endogenous. The 'risk' input, such as correlation and volatility are a function of a market which functions more like poker than roulette (i.e. the behavior of the other players matters).

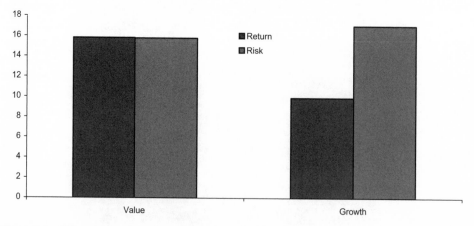

Figure 7.4   Risk and return for value and growth stocks (US, 1950–2008, %)
Source: SG Global Strategy research.

Risk shouldn't be defined as standard deviation (or volatility). I have never met a long-only investor who gives a damn about upside volatility. Risk is an altogether more complex topic — I have argued that a trinity of risk sums up the aspects that investors should be looking at. Valuation risk, business or earnings risk, and balance sheet risk (see Chapter 2).

Of course, under CAPM the proper measure of risk is beta. However, as Ben Graham pointed out, beta measures price variability, not risk. Beta is probably most often used by analysts in their calculations of the cost of capital, and indeed by CFOs in similar calculations. However, even here beta is unhelpful. Far from the theoretical upward-sloping relationship between risk and return, the evidence (including that collected by Fama and French) shows no relationship, and even arguably an inverse one from the model prediction.

This, of course, ignores the difficulties and vagaries of actually calculating beta. Do you use, daily, weekly or monthly data, and over what time period? The answers to these questions are non-trivial in their impact upon the analysts calculations. In a very recent paper, Fernandez and Bermejo showed that the best approach might simply be to assume that beta equals 1.0 for all stocks. (Another reminder that there are no points for elegance in this world!)

The EMH has also given us the Modigliani and Miller propositions on dividend irrelevance, and capital structure irrelevance. These concepts have both been used by unscrupulous practitioners to further their own causes. For instance, those in favor of repurchases over dividends, or even those in favor of retained earnings over distributed earnings, have effectively relied upon the M&M propositions to argue that shareholders should be indifferent to the way in which they receive their return (ignoring the inconvenient evidence that firms tend to waste their retained earnings, and that repurchases are far more transitory in nature than dividends).

Similarly, the M&M capital structure irrelevance proposition has encouraged corporate financiers and corporates themselves to gear up on debt. After all, according to this theory investors shouldn't care whether 'investment' is financed by retained earnings, equity issuance or debt issuance.

The EMH also gave rise to another fallacious distraction of our world — shareholder value. Ironically this started out as a movement to stop the focus on short-term earnings. Under EMH, the price of a company is, of course, just the net present value of all future cash flows. So focusing on maximizing the share price was exactly the same thing as maximizing future profitability. Unfortunately in a myopic world this all breaks down, and we end up with a quest to maximize short-term earnings!

But perhaps the most insidious aspect of the EMH is the way in which it has influenced the behavior of active managers in their pursuit of adding value. This might sound odd, but bear with me while I try to explain what might, upon cursory inspection, sound like an oxymoron.

All but the most diehard of EMH fans admit that there is a role for active management. After all, who else would keep the market efficient — a point first made by Grossman and Stigliz in their classic paper, 'The impossibility of the informational efficient market'. The extreme diehards probably wouldn't even tolerate this, but their arguments don't withstand the *reductio ad absurdum* that if the market were efficient, prices would of course be correct, and thus volumes should be equal to zero.

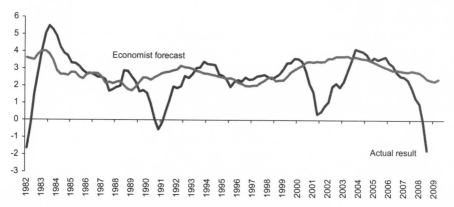

Figure 7.5   Economists are useless at forecasting — US GDP (%, 4q mav)
Source: SG Global Strategy research.

The EMH is pretty clear that active managers can add value via one of two routes. First there is inside information — which we will ignore today because it is generally illegal in most markets. Second, they could outperform if they could see the future more accurately than everyone else.

The EMH also teaches us that opportunities will be fleeting as someone will surely try to arbitrage them away. This, of course, is akin to the age old joke about the economist and his friend walking along the street. The friend points out a $100 bill lying on the pavement. The economist says, 'It isn't really there because, if it were, someone would have already picked it up.'

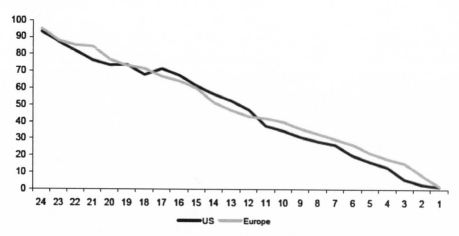

Figure 7.6   Forecast error over time: US and European markets 2001–2006 (%)
Source: SG Global Strategy research.

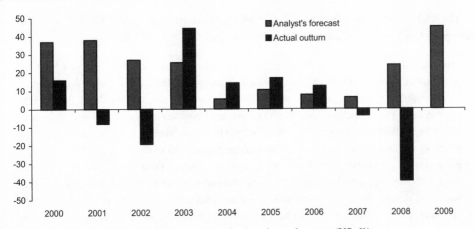

Figure 7.7   Analyst expected returns (via target prices) and actual returns (US, %)
Source: SG Global Strategy research.

Sadly these simple edicts are no joking matter as they are probably the most damaging aspects of the EMH legacy. Thus the EMH urges investors to try to forecast the future. In my opinion this is one of the biggest wastes of time, yet one that is nearly universal in our industry (Figure 7.5). About 80–90% of the investment processes that I come across revolve around forecasting. Yet there isn't a scrap of evidence to suggest that we can actually see the future at all (Figures 7.6 and 7.7).

The EMH's insistence on the fleeting nature of opportunities combined with the career risk that bedevils Homo Ovinus has led to an overt focus on the short term. This is typified by Figure 7.8 which shows the average holding period for a stock on the New York Stock Exchange. It is now just six months!

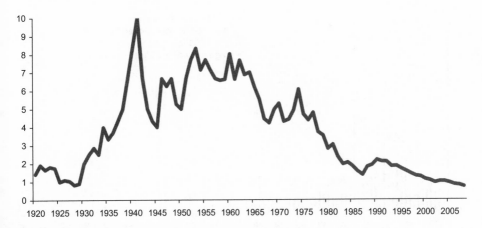

Figure 7.8   Average holding period for a stock on the NYSE (years)
Source: SG Global Strategy research.

The undue focus upon benchmark and relative performance also leads Homo Ovinus to engage in Keynes' beauty contest. As Keynes wrote:

> Professional investment may be likened to those newspaper competitions in which the competitors have to pick out the six prettiest faces from a hundred photographs, the price being awarded to the competitor whose choice most nearly corresponds to the average preference of the competitors as a whole; so that each competitor has to pick, not those faces which he himself finds prettiest, but those which he thinks likeliest to catch the fancy of the other competitors, all of whom are looking at the problem from the same point of view. It is not a case of choosing those which, to the best of one's judgment, are really prettiest, nor even those which average opinion genuinely thinks the prettiest. We have reached the third degree where we devote our intelligences to anticipating what average opinion expects the average opinion to be. And there are some, I believe, who practice the fourth, fifth and higher degrees.

This game can be easily replicated by asking people to pick a number between 0 and 100, and telling them that the winner will be the person who picks the number closest to two-thirds of the average number picked. Figure 7.9 shows the results from the largest incidence of the game that I have played — in fact the third largest game ever played, and the only one played purely among professional investors.

The highest possible correct answer is 67. To go for 67 you have to believe that every other muppet in the known universe has just gone for 100. The fact we got a whole raft of responses above 67 is more than slightly alarming.

You can see spikes which represent various levels of thinking. The spike at 50 represents what we (somewhat rudely) call level zero thinkers. They are the investment equivalent of Homer Simpson, 0, 100, duh 50! Not a vast amount of cognitive effort expended here!

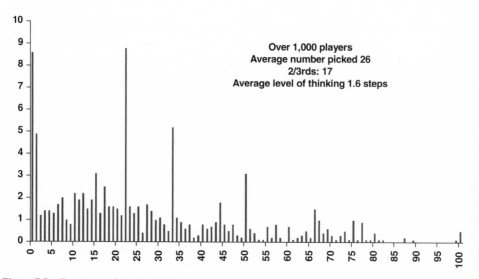

Figure 7.9 Frequency of choices in beauty contest game (%)
Source: SG Global Strategy research.

There is a spike at 33 — of those who expect everyone else in the world to be Homer. There's a spike at 22, again those who obviously think everyone else is at 33. As you can see there is also a spike at zero. Here we find all the economists, game theorists and mathematicians of the world. They are the only people trained to solve these problems backwards. And indeed the only stable Nash equilibrium is zero (two-thirds of zero is still zero). However, it is only the 'correct' answer when everyone chooses zero.

The final noticeable spike is at 1. These are economists who have (mistakenly . . .) been invited to one dinner party (economists only ever get invited to one dinner party). They have gone out into the world and realized that the rest of the world doesn't think like them. So they try to estimate the scale of irrationality. However, they end up suffering the curse of knowledge (once you know the true answer, you tend to anchor to it). In this game, which is fairly typical, the average number picked was 26, giving a two-thirds average of 17. Just three people out of more than 1,000 picked the number 17.

I play this game to try to illustrate just how hard it is to be just one step ahead of everyone else — to get in before everyone else, and get out before everyone else. Yet despite this fact, this seems to be exactly what a large number of investors spend their time doing.

PRIMA FACIE CASE AGAINST EMH: FOREVER BLOWING BUBBLES

Let me now turn to the prima facie case against the EMH. Oddly enough it is one that doesn't attract much attention in academia. As Larry Summers pointed out in his wonderful parody of financial economics, 'Traditional finance is more concerned with checking that two 8oz bottles of ketchup is close to the price of one 16oz bottle, than in understanding the price of the 16oz bottle.'

The first stock exchange was founded in 1602. The first equity bubble occurred just 118 years later — the South Sea bubble. Since then we have encountered bubbles with an alarming regularity. My friends at GMO define a bubble as a (real) price movement that is at least two-standard-deviations from trend. Now a two-standard-deviation event should occur roughly every 44 years. Yet since 1925, GMO have found a staggering 30-plus bubbles. That is equivalent to slightly more than one every three years!

In my own work I've examined the patterns that bubbles tend to follow. By looking at some of the major bubbles in history (including the South Sea bubble, the railroad bubble of the 1840s, the Japanese bubble of the late 1980s, and the NASDAQ bubble[2]), I have been able to extract the following underlying pattern (Figure 7.10). Bubbles inflate over the course of around three years, with an almost parabolic explosion in prices towards the peak of the bubble. Then without exception they deflate. This bursting is generally slightly more rapid than the inflation, taking around two years.

---

[2]Two economists have written a paper arguing that the NASDAQ bubble might not have been a bubble after all — only an academic with no experience of the real world could ever posit such a thing.

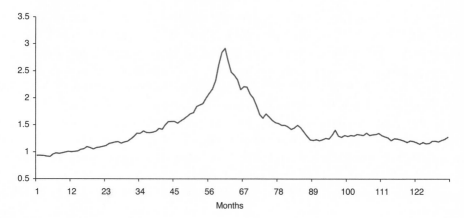

Figure 7.10   Our Bubble Index
Source: SG Global Strategy research.

While the details and technicalities of each episode are different, the underlying dynamics follow a very similar pattern. As Mark Twain put it, 'History doesn't repeat but it does rhyme'. Indeed the first well-documented analysis of the underlying patterns of bubbles that I can find is a paper by J.S. Mills in 1867. He lays out a framework that is very close to the Minsky/Kindleberger model that I have used for years to understand the inflation and deflation of bubbles. This makes it hard to understand why so many among the learned classes seem to believe that you can't identify a bubble before it bursts. To my mind the clear existence and ex-ante diagnosis of bubbles represent by far and away the most compelling evidence of the gross inefficiency of markets.

THE EMH 'NUCLEAR BOMB'

Now as a behavioralist I am constantly telling people to beware of confirmatory bias — the habit of looking for information that agrees with you. So in an effort to avert the accusation that I am guilty of failing to allow for my own biases (something I've done before), I will now turn to the evidence that the EMH fans argue is the strongest defense of their belief — the simple fact that active management doesn't outperform. Mark Rubinstein describes this as the nuclear bomb of the EMH, and says that we behavioralists have nothing in our arsenal to match it, our evidence of inefficiencies and irrationalities amounts to puny rifles.

However, I will argue that this viewpoint is flawed both theoretically and empirically. The logical error is a simple one. It is to confuse the absence of evidence with evidence of the absence. That is to say, if the EMH leads active investors to focus on the wrong sources of performance (i.e. forecasting), then it isn't any wonder that active management won't be able to outperform.

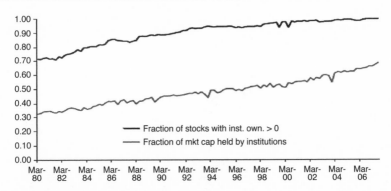

Figure 7.11   Institutional Ownership, US 1980–2007 (%)
Source: Lewellen (2009).

Empirically, the 'nuclear bomb' is also suspect. I want to present two pieces of evidence that highlight the suspect nature of the EMH claim. The first is work by Jonathan Lewellen of Dartmouth College.

In a recent paper, Lewellen looked at the aggregate holdings of US institutional investors over the period 1980–2007. He finds that essentially they hold the market portfolio. To some extent this isn't a surprise, as the share of institutional ownership has risen steadily over time from around 30% in 1980 to almost 70% at the end of 2007 (Figure 7.11). This confirms the zero sum game aspect of active management (or negative sum, after costs) and also the validity of Keynes' observation that it (the market) is professional investors trying to outsmart each other.

However, Lewellen also shows that, in aggregate, institutions don't try to outperform! He sorts stocks into quintiles based on a variety of characteristics and then compares the fraction of the institutional portfolio invested in each (relative to institutions' investment in all five quintiles) with the quintile's weight in the market portfolio (the quintile's market cap relative to the market cap of all five quintiles) — i.e. he measures the weight institutional investors place on a characteristic relative to the weight the market places on each trait.

Figure 7.12 shows the results for a sample of the characteristics that Lewellen used. With the exception of size, the aggregate institutional portfolio barely deviates from the market weights. So institutions aren't even really trying to tilt their portfolios towards the factors we know generate outperformance over the long term.

Lewellen concludes:

Quite simply, institutions overall seem to do little more than hold the market portfolio, at least from the standpoint of their pre-cost and pre-fee returns. Their aggregate portfolio almost perfectly mimics the value-weighted index, with a market beta of 1.01 and an economically small, precisely estimated CAPM alpha of 0.08% quarterly. Institutions overall take essentially no bet on any of the most important stock characteristics known

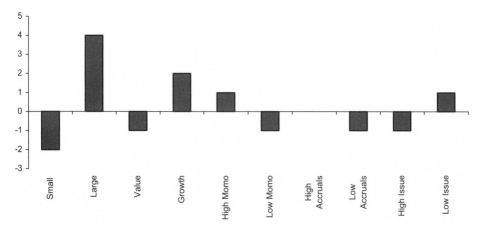

Figure 7.12   Institutional investors vs US market (weight differences)
Source: Lewellen (2009).

to predict returns, like book-to-market, momentum, or accruals. The implication is that, to the extent that institutions deviate from the market portfolio, they seem to bet primarily on idiosyncratic returns — bets that aren't particularly successful. Another implication is that institutions, in aggregate, don't exploit anomalies in the way they should if they rationally tried to maximize the (pre-cost) mean variance trade-off of their portfolios, either relative or absolute.

Put into our terms, institutions are more worried about career risk (losing your job) or business risk (losing funds under management) than they are about doing the right thing!

The second piece of evidence I'd like to bring to your attention is a paper by Randy Cohen, Christopher Polk and Bernhard Silli. They examined the 'best ideas' of US fund managers over the period 1991–2005. 'Best ideas' are measured as the biggest difference between the managers' holdings and the weights in the index.

The performance of these best ideas is impressive. Focusing on the top 25% of best ideas across the universe of active managers, Cohen *et al.* find that the average return is over 19% per annum against a market return of 12% per annum That is to say, the stocks in which the managers display most confidence outperformed the market by a significant degree.

The corollary to this is that the other stocks they hold are dragging down their performance. Hence it appears that the focus on relative performance — and the fear of underperformance against an arbitrary benchmark — is a key source of underperformance.

At an anecdotal level I have never quite recovered from discovering that a value manager at a large fund was made to operate with a 'completion portfolio'. This was a euphemism for an add-on to the manager's selected holdings that essentially made his fund behave much more like the index!

As Cohen *et al.* conclude, 'The poor overall performance of mutual fund managers in the past is not due to a lack of stock-picking ability, but rather to institutional factors that encourage them to over-diversify.' Thus, as Sir John Templeton said, 'It is impossible to produce a superior performance unless you do something different from the majority.'

The bottom line is that the EMH nuclear bomb is more of a party popper than a weapon of mass destruction. The EMH would have driven Sherlock Holmes to despair. As Holmes opined, 'It is a capital mistake to theorize before one has data. Insensibly one begins to twist facts to suit theories, instead of theories to suit facts.'

The EMH, as Shiller puts it, is 'one of the most remarkable errors in the history of economic thought'. EMH should be consigned to the dustbin of history. We need to stop teaching it, and brainwashing the innocent. Rob Arnott tells a lovely story of a speech he was giving to some 200 finance professors. He asked how many of them taught EMH — pretty much everyone's hand was up. Then he asked how many of them believed in it. Only two hands remained up!

A similar sentiment seems to have been expressed by the recent CFA UK survey which revealed that 67% of respondents thought that the market failed to behave rationally. When a journalist asked me what I thought of this, I simply said, 'About bloody time.' However, 76% said that behavioral finance wasn't yet sufficiently robust to replace modern portfolio theory (MPT) as the basis of investment thought. This is, of course, utter nonsense. Successful investors existed long before EMH and MPT. Indeed, the vast majority of successful long-term investors are value investors who reject most of the precepts of EMH and MPT.

Will we ever be successful at finally killing off the EMH? I am a pessimist. As Jeremy Grantham said when asked what investors would learn from this crisis: 'In the short term, a lot. In the medium term, a little. In the long term, nothing at all. That is the historical precedent.' Or, as JK Galbraith put it, markets are characterized by 'Extreme brevity of financial memory. . . There can be few fields of human endeavor in which history counts for so little as in the world of finance.'

8

Pseudoscience and Finance: The Tyranny of Numbers and the Fallacy of Safety[1]

In the world of modern finance, a love of numbers has replaced a desire for critical thinking. As long as something has a number attached to it, it is taken as gospel truth. Research shows that people are often fooled by the use of pseudoscience. Simply making things sound complex makes people believe them more! Risk managers, analysts and consultants are all guilty of using pseudoscience to promote an illusion of safety. We all need to be on our guard against the artificial deployment of meaningless numbers. Critical thinking and skepticism are the most unrated (and scarce) tools in our world.

- A recent study by Weisberg *et al.* revealed just how easily most of us are fooled by anything that sounds vaguely scientific. They put neuroscience language into a standard psychological explanation for a variety of biases. Some of these explanations were 'good' (genuine) and some were 'bad' (circular restatements of the bias itself). Both good and bad explanations were rated as much better when they contained the meaningless neuroscience information.
- Garner *et al.* have shown that people are easily distracted by 'seductive details'. After reading just a few paragraphs loaded with 'interesting' but irrelevant information, people simply can't recall the important stuff! Suddenly the world of analysts is starting to make some sense to me!
- Finance is loaded with pseudoscience and seductive details. For instance, risk management is clearly pseudoscience of the highest order. Numbers like Value at Risk (VaR) are used to create comfort, but actually just generate the illusion of safety. The presence of fat tails, endogenous correlations and risks of using trailing input all combine to render VaR impotent. It is no surprise that the mea maxima culpa from UBS cited overreliance on VaR as one of the core problems.
- Analysts are also guilty of using pseudoscience. They are providers of seductive details. Read most analysts' reports and they are full of 'interesting' but irrelevant information. The idea that forecasting earnings to two decimal places over the next five years is surely laughable. It has no merit. All the more so with the latest reporting season revealing the biggest overestimation of profits growth ever recorded!

---

[1]This article appeared in *Mind Matters* on 29 April 2008. Copyright © 2008 by The Société Générale Group. All rights reserved. The material discussed was accurate at the time of publication.

- Performance measurement is another example of the reign of pseudoscience in finance. Weasel words such as alpha, beta and tracking error are used to promote confusion in this arena. Style drift, holding-based style analysis, and returns-based style analysis are all used to make the industry sound important. But all are seriously flawed when it comes to the meaning behind the numbers.
- Simply because something can be quantified doesn't mean that it is sensible. There is no substitute for rigorous critical or skeptical thinking. Blind faith in numbers for numbers' sake is a path to ruin.

In the world of modern finance, a love of numbers has replaced a desire for critical thinking. This is a highly regrettable trend. Don't get me wrong, I am a big fan of using empirical evidence to ascertain the truth of many of the wild claims that seem to circulate in our industry (a process I have called Evidence Based Investing). However, all too often we seem to take pseudoscience as gospel truth, accepting anything with a number as a fact.

BLINDED BY PSEUDOSCIENCE

A recent study by Weisberg *et al.* (2008) revealed some intriguing findings about the way in which we can be blinded by pseudoscience and just how gullible we are when it comes to pseudoscientific explanations.

In their clever experiment, Weisberg *et al.* (2008) gave three groups of people (naïve students, students in neuroscience, and experts) a set of descriptions of psychological phenomena which varied along two dimensions: (i) the quality of the explanation and (ii) the use of neuroscience.

A sample discussing the curse of knowledge can be found in Table 8.1. In all cases the 'good' explanations were genuine explanations that had been given by researchers. The 'bad' explanations are simply circular restatements of the phenomenon, with no explanatory power at all.

Table 8.1   The curse of knowledge

	Good explanation	Bad explanation
Without neuroscience	The researchers claim that this 'curse' happens because subjects have trouble switching their point of view to consider what someone else might know, mistakenly projecting their own knowledge onto others.	The researchers claim that this 'curse' happens because subjects make more mistakes when they have to judge the knowledge of others. People are much better at judging what they themselves know.
With neuroscience	Brain scans indicate that this 'curse' happens because of the frontal lobe brain circuitry, known to be involved in self-knowledge. Subjects have trouble switching their point of view to consider what someone else might know, mistakenly projecting their own knowledge onto others.	Brain scans indicate that this 'curse' happens because of the frontal lobe brain circuitry, known to be involved in self-knowledge. Subjects make more mistakes when they have to judge the knowledge of others. People are much better at judging what they themselves know.

Source: Weisberg *et al.* (2008).

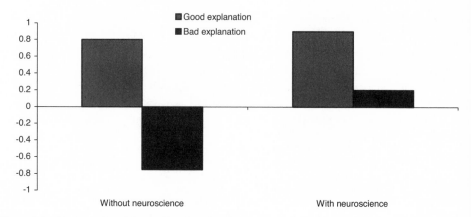

Figure 8.1   Novice rating of the quality of explanation
Source: Weisberg *et al.* (2008).

For the 'with neuroscience' condition, information on an area of the brain known to be involved with the general sort of phenomena under discussion was inserted. However, because this was already known, it shouldn't have any impact upon the perceived validity of the explanation.

Participants were asked to rate the explanations of the phenomena, and told that in some cases they would be reading false explanations. They rated the explanations on a 7-point scale from –3 (very unsatisfactory explanation) to +3 (very satisfactory explanation).

Figures 8.1, 8.2, 8.3 show the results obtained across the three different groups. The novices (those without any training in psychology or neuroscience) did a pretty good job of telling good explanations from bad in the absence of neuroscience information (Figure 8.1). However, as soon as that was added, it markedly impaired their ability to tell good explanations from bad.

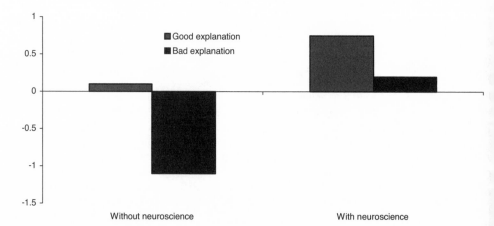

Figure 8.2   Student ratings of the quality of explanation
Source: Weisberg *et al.* (2008).

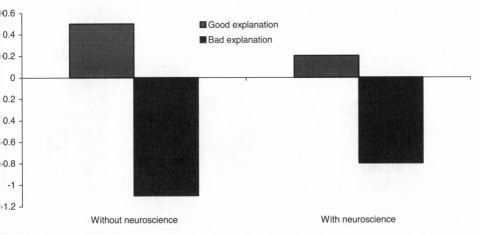

Figure 8.3 Expert ratings of the quality of explanation
Source: Weisberg *et al.* (2008).

In particular bad explanations with a neuroscience element were rated as much better than bad explanations without any neuroscience language.

The second group comprised the students taking courses in intermediate level cognitive neuroscience. These students should have learned about the basic logic and construct of neuroscience experiments. However, Figure 8.2 shows that their responses weren't significantly different from the novice group. They seemed to place heavy weight on neuroscience input, downplaying the good explanation in its absence! Bad explanations were once again boosted by the presence of neuroscience information. It seems as if these students were only interested in the item they were studying.

The third and final group were 'experts' — characterized by advanced degrees in cognitive neuroscience or cognitive psychology. This group showed different behavior to the previous two. As Figure 8.3 shows, this group discriminated between good and bad explanations in the absence of neuroscience. It also appears that when faced with needless information on neuroscience, this group marked down good explanations. Effectively they punished explanations that used pointless neuroscience. This finding also confirms that the neuroscience information itself had no value.

WATCHING TV IMPROVES YOUR MATH ABILITY

Another example of this form of pseudoscientific blindness can be found in McCabe and Castel (2008). They had participants read three brief articles, each summarizing the results of fictitious brain-imaging studies. The articles made claims that were not necessitated by the data, giving participants some basis for skepticism in their ratings of the soundness of the argument.

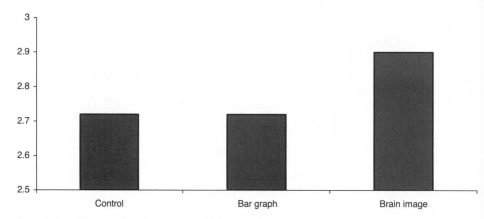

Figure 8.4 Rating of scientific reasoning (1 = low, 4 = high)
Source: McCabe and Castel (2007).

One article argued that 'Watching TV is related to maths ability'. It concluded that because watching television and completing arithmetic problems both led to activation in the temporal lobe, watching television improved math skills. This similarity in activation was depicted in a bar graph or brain image, or was only explained in the text. Each article was approximately 300 words long, presented on a single page, with the image embedded in the text.

After reading each article, participants were asked to rate if the scientific reasoning in the article made sense. Responses were made on a four-point scale, with response options including 'strongly disagree', 'disagree', 'agree', and 'strongly agree' (coded 1, 2, 3 or 4, respectively).

Figure 8.4 presents the ratings as a function of the image shown to participants. Yet again participants were fooled by the presence of the brain image. Studies that showed such a picture were rated as much more scientifically sound!

SEDUCTIVE DETAILS

In general, these findings fit into a larger body of work concerned with 'seductive details'. In a paper written in 1989, Ruth Garner and colleagues first noticed that people were often distracted by 'interesting' but 'uninformative' noise. In their test, people were given three paragraphs to read, such as:

> Some insects live alone, some live in big colonies. Wasps that live alone are called solitary wasps. The Mud Dauber wasp is a solitary wasp. The Click beetle lives alone. When a Click beetle is on its back, it flips itself into the air, and lands right side up whilst making a clicking noise. Ants live in big colonies.

It is fairly obvious that the important information is the first sentence. The story about the Click beetle is interesting but not important. Some of the participants were given paragraphs with just the important information in them, other received paragraphs like the one above.

Having read the paragraphs, subjects were then asked to recall the important information contained within the text they had read. The ability to recall the important information was massively determined by whether the paragraph had contained seductive details or not. Of those reading the paragraphs that contained just the important facts, 93% could recall the important generalizations. Of those faced with paragraphs containing seductive details, only 43% could recall the important elements!

APPLICATIONS TO FINANCE

Risk Management

Over the years I have been a vocal critic of risk management. It is a prime example of the way in which we can be blinded by numbers. It is comforting to be presented with a number that represents the Value at Risk (VaR), but it is also almost totally meaningless. The illusion of safety is created by false belief in the infallibility of numbers.

VaR is fundamentally flawed — after all it cuts off the very bit of the distribution that we are interested in: the tails! This is akin to buying a car with an airbag that is guaranteed to work unless you have a crash. It also ignores the fact that risk is endogenous, not exogenous, within many financial applications. The entire risk management industry is an example of pseudoscience: people pretending to measure and quantify things that just can't be measured or quantified.

My favorite recent analysis of the failure of VaR came from a speech given by Dave Einhorn (2008):

> By ignoring the tails, Value at Risk creates an incentive to take excessive but remote risks. Consider an investment in a coin-flip. If you bet $100 on tails at even money, your VaR to a 99% threshold is $100, as you will lose that amount 50% of the time, which is obviously within the threshold. In this case the VaR will equal the maximum loss.
>
> Compare that to a bet where you offer 217 to 1 odds on $100 that heads won't come up seven times in a row. You will win more than 99.2% of the time, which exceeds the 99% threshold. As a result, your 99% VaR is zero even though you are exposed to a possible $21,700 loss. In other words, an investment bank wouldn't have to put up any capital to make this bet.

In the light of this analysis, it isn't a surprise that the recently published catalogue of errors that UBS confessed (*see UBS Shareholder Report on UBS's Write-Downs*) contained yet another mea culpa on the use of VaR:

> Time series reliance: The historical time series used to drive VaR and Stress are based on five years of data, whereby the data was sourced from a period of relatively positive growth. Regular work being performed during the relevant period focused on confirming the efficacy of existing scenarios based on broad-based economic developments and historical events. When updates to methodologies were presented to Group and IB Senior Management, hindsight suggests that these updates did not attribute adequate weight to

the significant growth in the US housing market and especially the subprime market. The Market Risk function did not develop scenarios that were based on more fundamental attributes of the US housing market.

Lack of Housing Market Risk Factor Loss limits: In a similar vein, it appears that no attempt was made to develop an RFL structure that captured more meaningful attributes related to the US housing market generally, such as defaults, loan to value ratios or other similar attributes to statistically shock the existing portfolio.

Overreliance on VaR and Stress: MRC relied on VaR and Stress numbers, even though delinquency rates were increasing and origination standards were falling in the US mortgage market. It continued to do so throughout the build-up of significant positions in subprime assets that were only partially hedged. Presentations of MRC representatives to UBS's senior governance bodies did not provide adequate granularity of subprime positions UBS held in its various businesses. No warnings were given to Group Senior Management about the limitations of the presented numbers or the need to look at the broader contextual framework and the findings were not challenged with perseverance.

The presence of fat tails, endogenous correlations and risks of trailing inputs have been known for years. Yet despite this people continue to use such methods, arguing that something is better than nothing. However, we must consider if some medicine is really better than no medicine, especially if the wrong treatment can kill you. This misplaced faith in pseudoscience has once again extracted a high price.

Analysts and their Addiction to Numbers

However, risk managers aren't alone in deploying pseudoscience. Analysts are guilty too. They are providers of seductive details. The idea that forecasting earnings to two decimal places over the next five years has any merit is surely laughable. Bear in mind that the 2000 or so analysts employed on the Street have recently displayed just how truly appalling they are at forecasting

At the start of the third quarter of 2007, average estimates called for US earnings to increase by 5.7%. By the end of the quarter, analysts had cut by more than half to 2.7%. Companies ended up reporting a 2.5% drop in profits. Analysts were 8.2 percentage points too high!

Forecasts for the fourth quarter were even worse. Analysts predicted 10.9% growth before flipping the projection to a decline of 7.9%. S&P 500 companies reported that profit dropped 22.6%, resulting in an overestimation of profits growth by 33.5 percentage points, the biggest miss ever (Figure 8.5).

Not to worry, of course, as analysts say, everything will be alright by the second half of the year. They have pencilled in earnings declines of 11.3% and 3.5% in 2008's first and second quarters, but then a recovery occurs with a 13.9% rise in the third quarter and a jump to 54.5% in the fourth quarter!

Do clients really value this kind of useless noise? Surely not. But whenever one asks analysts why they persist in producing this kind of rubbish, the invariable response is that their clients want it. Could it be that the buy-side has fallen for the pseudoscience and its seductive details?

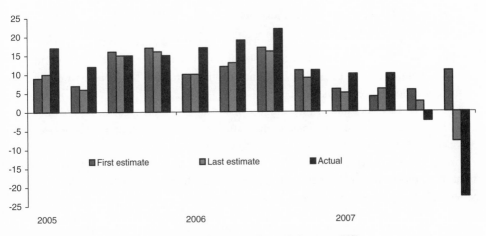

Figure 8.5   Who needs analysts? Recent performance of growth forecasts (US)
Source: Bloomberg.

My conversations with buy-siders tend to suggest not. The fund managers I speak to generally ignore the meaningless noise generated by analysts in terms of their forecasts, preferring instead to focus on analysts who are doing something different. But perhaps I have a biased sample!

Indeed, as I was going to print I came across a study by Bryan Armstrong of Ashton Partners seeking to explore the importance of sell-side estimates for buy-side institutions. Of the 30 portfolio managers surveyed, every single one stated that consensus estimates (Figure 8.6) were important to their investment decision-making process! Now I'm really worried.

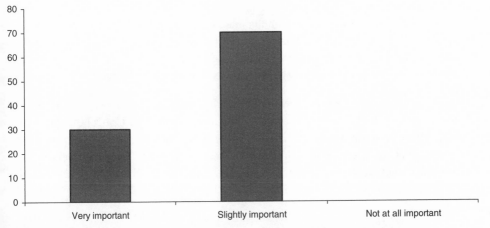

Figure 8.6   Percentage of portfolio managers saying consensus estimates were important
Source: Ashton Partners.

Performance Measurement as Pseudoscience

The final application of pseudoscience that I wish to vent about in this note is performance measurement. This is surely another example of too much faith being placed in one number (or a few numbers at best). Alpha, beta and tracking error are the weasel words used to promote pseudoscience in this arena.

The use of such measures as tracking error for an active manager is akin to sending a boxer into the ring with instructions to make sure he is always within a point or two of his opponent, rather than with the aim of trying to win the bout.

Another aspect of the pseudoscience nature of performance measurement was brought home to me recently as I read an intriguing new paper by John Minahan (2009) on 'investment beliefs.' He describes the following situation:

> I was new to the industry . . . [a] manager came to my attention because she showed up in a holdings-based style analysis having migrated from value to growth, and this set off alarms regarding 'style discipline'. The manager had very good performance, and this happened during a period of time when growth was outperforming value, so on the surface it looked like the manager had broken her value discipline because growth was where the returns were.
>
> A closer examination of the portfolio revealed that the manager had very little turnover during this period, and that the stocks which were now plotting as growth had plotted as value when the manager bought them. All that had really happened was that the manager was correct with many of these stocks: earnings were up and prices even more, and stocks started plotting as growth stocks. She was able to explain the original investment thesis for any stock I asked about, and for those she still held, justify that the thesis was still intact. This led me to suspect that the style-box program I was using just wasn't subtle enough to accurately capture the manager's style, and that the style was in fact consistent through this period.
>
> When I discussed my concerns with the more senior consultant with whom I worked on this account, he dismissed my interpretation. He claimed that the style analyzer was 'objective' whereas the manager's explanation was 'spin'. He told me that when I got a little more experience I will learn to be more skeptical of charming managers.

The senior consultant here is exceptionally guilty of blind faith in pseudoscience. Just because something is quantitative doesn't mean that it is infallible. Critical thought is still required. Minahan was most likely correct in his analysis. Indeed Fama and French (2007) have shown that much of the value premium comes from stocks that effectively migrate across 'style boundaries' (see Table 8.2).

Table 8.2   Migration across styles (US 1927–2006)

	Portfolio	Minus	Same	Plus	Changed Size
Average Excess Returns					
Big Growth	−0.9	−12.0	0.8	15.6	−37.4
Big Neutral	1.2	−11.5	0.4	16.6	−31.1
Big Value	4.8	−36.3	3.2	16.9	−31.7
Average Transition Probability					
Big Growth		10.9	87.5	0.7	0.9
Big Neutral		8.6	75.1	15	1.2
Big Value		0.1	75.2	22.5	2.2
Average Contribution to Portfolio's Excess Returns					
Big Growth		−1.2	0.6	0.1	−0.4
Big Neutral		−0.9	0.3	2.2	−0.4
Big Value		0	2.3	3.3	−0.7

Source: Fama and French (2007).

CONCLUSIONS

As a fan of an empirical approach to finance it saddens me when I come across pseudoscience in finance. However, it is all too common. Blind faith in anything containing numbers is the curse of our industry. We need to seek to develop a more critical/skeptical mindset if we are to avoid stumbling into the seductive details of a pseudoscientific approach to our field.

Numbers don't constitute safety. Just because a risk manager tells you that the VaR is X, it doesn't mean a thing. Nor for that matter does an analyst saying that company Y is trading on a $Y \times 2010$ earnings, or a consultant saying that a fund manager was 3% alpha. All these need to be put in context. When critically appraised, all of these are likely to be classed as pseudoscience. The artificial deployment of meaningless numbers to generate the illusion of safety is something that we must all guard against.

9

Bonds: Speculation Not Investment[1]

It isn't often that Albert and I find ourselves on opposing sides of an investment debate. However, the current state of the government bond market has us divided. From my perspective as a long-term value-oriented investor, bonds simply don't offer any value. They already price in the US slipping into Japanese-style prolonged deflation. However, they offer no protection at all if (and it may be a big if) the Fed can succeed in reintroducing inflation (what Keynes described as the 'euthanasia of the rentier'[2]). There may be a 'speculative' case for continuing to hold bonds, but there isn't an investment case.

- To my mind, in principle, government bond valuation is relatively simple. I see the value as the summation of three components: the real yield, expected inflation, and an inflation risk premium. The market tells us that the real yield for 10-year US government bonds is around 2%. Given that the nominal yield is also around 2% at the moment, the market is implying that inflation will be around 0% per annum over the next 10 years.
- This suggests that the market believes that the US will follow the Japanese path into slow grinding deflation. Unravelling the forward curve shows the market expecting 10y bonds to yield 3% in 10 years time! Surveys of long-term expectations show a different picture — they suggest that inflation will be around 2.5% per annum over the next 10 years. This implies a radically different pricing of bonds. In a normal world, a 'fair value' for US government bonds would be around 4.5–4.75%.
- However, this isn't a normal world. The US has become enormously over-leveraged. If deflation were to take hold, then debt deflation dynamics would be unleashed which would have truly horrible consequences for the economy. It is all too easy to see the bursting of the credit bubble causing a tsunami of deflation to sweep through the system.
- It took Japan seven years after its first encounter with deflation to instigate quantitative easing; the US has started before deflation is actually here. Bernanke clearly believes that monetary policy is far from impotent at the zero bound. When talking to Japanese policy makers in 2000 he argued that measures such as money financed transfer (printing cash to pay for tax cuts), inflation targets and unconventional measures were all available even with interest rates at zero.

---

[1]This article appeared in *Mind Matters* on 6 January 2009. Copyright © 2009 by The Société Générale Group. All rights reserved. The material discussed was accurate at the time of publication.

[2]A rentier is one who lives off rent/income i.e. the bond holder.

- What happens when an irresistible force hits an immovable object? I haven't a clue, and neither does any one else. However, the government bond market has clearly opted to believe in deflation. Thus if the Fed is successful then bonds offer no protection at all. The 'euthanasia of the rentier' will ensue.

- Ben Graham said, 'An investment operation is one which, upon thorough analysis, promises safety of principal and a satisfactory return. Operations not meeting these requirements are speculative.' Bonds simply don't offer a satisfactory return (or indeed a safety of principal) at current yield levels. They, as Jim Grant put it, may well be 'return-free risk'. A speculative case of bond holding can still be made. In a myopic world, it may be possible to ride the news flow down. However, I am an investor not a speculator. So government bonds have no place in my portfolio.

t isn't often that Albert and I find ourselves on opposite sides of the debate. In fact in the
ast eight years I can't recall a single occurrence of such an event. Indeed I am not even sure
hat we have a truly deep divide at the moment; it may merely be a matter of time horizon
und investment approach.

I tend to view the world through the lens of a long-term value-oriented absolute-return
nvestor. Albert is often more willing to tolerate momentum-driven shorter term positions
believe it or not!). Perhaps it is these differences in approach that have led to us to adopt
lifferent positions on the merits of holding government bonds. In the interest of adding to
he debate I will present the value-based bear-case here.

A LONG-TERM VIEW OF BONDS

Figure 9.1 shows the long-term history of US 10-year (or nearest equivalent) government
lebt. Over the very long-term the yield has averaged just over 4.5%. The figure makes it
clear how anomalous the inflationary experience of the 1970s was. However, current yields
are rapidly approaching all-time lows.

Of course, simply because yields are close to all-time lows isn't necessarily a sell signal.
Witness the example of Japan. Figure 9.2 shows the long-term picture for Japanese 10-year
government debt. I was working in Tokyo in 1995 and remembering thinking that as yields
reached 3%, surely they couldn't go any lower. Of course, they went on to halve, and then
halve again.

INTRINSIC VALUE FOR BONDS

How should one think about valuing bonds? I always have a simplistic view of the returns
to a government bond holder. I generally view bonds as having three components: the real
yield, expected inflation, and an inflation risk premium.

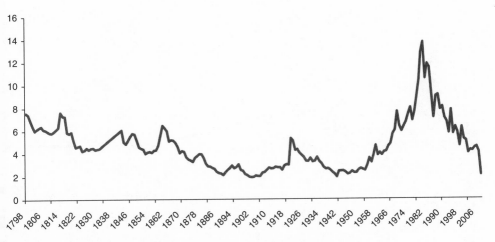

Figure 9.1   US 10-year government bond yields — a long-term perspective
Source: Homer, S. and Sylla, R. (2005).

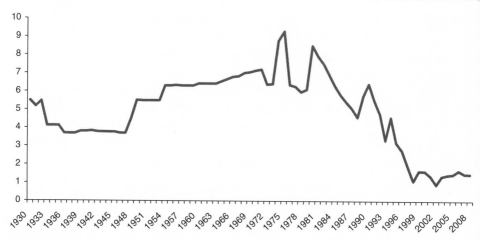

Figure 9.2   Japanese 10-year government bond yields — a long-term perspective
Source: Homer and Sylla (2005).

The real yield is generally said to be roughly equal to the long-term real growth rate (effectively creating an equilibrium condition between the marginal cost of capital and the marginal benefit of capital). Empirically this may be a dubious assumption as real yields and growth don't always enjoy a tight relationship, but it will do as a rough approximation. Of course, thanks to the use of index-linked (or inflation-protected) securities we have a live market in the real yield for many countries. In the US, 10-year TIPs are yielding around 2%.

Expected inflation is the second component in our simple approach to bond valuation. This can be assessed in several ways. For instance, surveys such as the survey of professional forecasters (almost certainly an oxymoron) ask respondents to assess the expected inflation rate over the next 10 years. Figure 9.3 shows the expected inflation rate per annum over

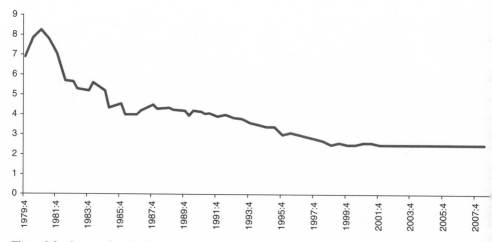

Figure 9.3   Survey of professional forecasters 10-year inflation expectation (% per annum)
Source: SG Equity Strategy research.

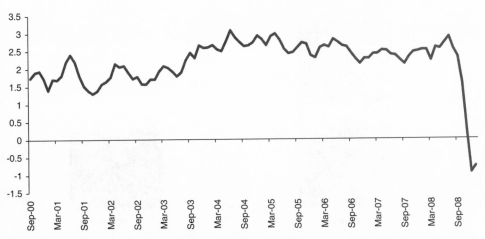

Figure 9.4   Implied inflation from nominal bonds minus TIPS (% per annum)
Source: SG Equity Strategy research.

the next 10 years according to this survey. At the risk of sounding like the Fed, inflation expectations remain surprisingly tightly anchored at 2.5% per annum.

In contrast, the market is pricing in a very different view (Figure 9.4). The gap between nominal bonds and TIPS gives a simple measure of implied inflation. With both groups of bonds yielding pretty much 2%, investors are implying zero inflation on a 10-year view!

Alternatively one can use inflation swaps to gain insight into the markets' pricing of future inflation (Figure 9.5). These instruments are now implying an inflation rate of just over 1.6% per annum for the next ten years. It is noteworthy just how recent the collapse in implied inflation has been!

Figure 9.5   10-year inflation swap implied inflation (% per annum)
Source: SG Equity Strategy research.

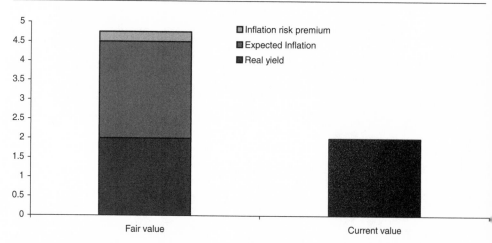

Figure 9.6   Rough fair-value bond benchmark vs actual yield
Source: SG Equity Strategy research.

The final component of our simple bond valuation approach is an inflation risk premium. Because inflation is obviously uncertain, a risk premium to compensate for the uncertainty is required. Although hard to estimate, current academic work suggests a range of somewhere from 25 to 50 bps might be regarded as normal.

PUTTING IT ALL TOGETHER

Using this simple approach to a bond valuation yields Figure 9.6. A 'fair value' under 'normal' inflation rates would be somewhere around 4.75%. Today's yields at a fraction over 2% are woefully short of the estimated fair value under 'normal' conditions.

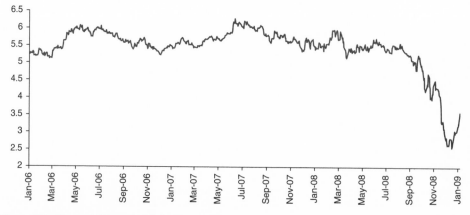

Figure 9.7   Forward 10-year bonds in 10 years' time
Source: SG Equity Strategy research.

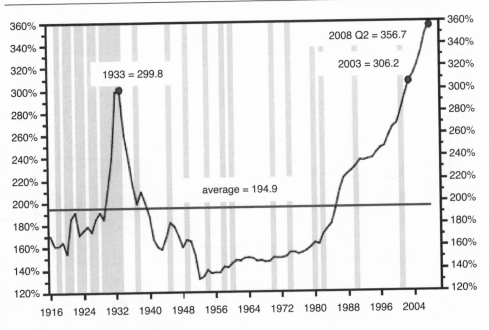

Figure 9.8   US total debt to GDP ratio
Source: Hoisington Investment Management.

Even if we unravel the forward curve we find that the market thinks that 10-year bonds in 10 years' time will yield just 3% (Figure 9.7). The markets seem convinced that low yields are here to stay for a prolonged period.

INFLATION OR DEFLATION

As I have written many times before, I am torn on the issue of the inflation/deflation debate. History teaches us that bursting credit bubbles unleash massive deflationary impulses on an economy. With the US economy facing an enormous debt overhang, and the US consumer engaged in its first retrenchment in a quarter of a century, it is easy to see the dangers of debt deflation (Figure 9.8).

However, the Fed's reaction to the deflationary threat has been enormous. The quantitative and qualitative easing that the Fed has embarked upon is truly unprecedented. We are now in a brave new world of monetary experimentation (Figure 9.9).

Whether or not the Fed is successful in staving off inflation is certainly beyond my knowledge. Bernanke has made his game plan for avoiding deflation exceptionally clear. He will do whatever he can to prevent deflation occurring in the US. In a speech given in 2000 to Japanese policy-makers Bernanke clearly acknowledged the greater threat that deflation posed in a highly leveraged economy, 'Zero inflation or mild deflation is potentially more dangerous in the modern environment than it was, say, in the classical gold standard era. The modern economy makes much heavier use of credit, especially longer-term credit, than the economies of the nineteenth century.'

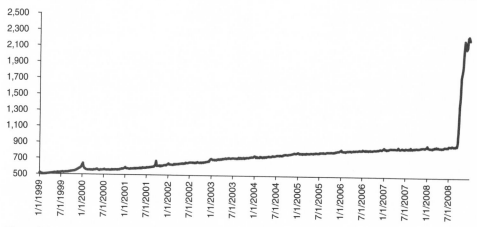

Figure 9.9   Fed's bastardization of the balance sheet (US$bn)
Source: SG Equity Strategy research.

Bernanke clearly believes that monetary policy is far from impotent at the zero interest-rate bound. In essence his argument is an arbitrage-based[3] one as follows:

> Money, unlike other forms of government debt, pays zero interest and has infinite maturity. The monetary authorities can issue as much money as they like. Hence, if the price level were truly independent of money issuance, then the monetary authorities could use the money they create to acquire indefinite quantities of goods and assets. This is manifestly impossible in equilibrium. Therefore money issuance must ultimately raise the price level, even if nominal interest rates are bounded at zero.

In the speech he laid out a menu of policy options that are available to the monetary authorities at the zero bound. First, aggressive currency depreciation — this is obviously less of an option for the US than it was for Japan, given the state of the rest of the world. Such a policy today would seem to be in danger of unleashing a 'beggar-thy-neighbor'/competitive devaluation response. Of course, this kind of policy is also more difficult when a great deal of overseas investors own your debt, and you don't want them to dump treasuries.

Second on Bernanke's list (although so far absent from the US response) is the introduction of an inflation target to help to mold the public's expectations about the central bank's desire for inflation. He mentions the range of 3-4%!

Third on the list was money-financed transfers. Essentially tax cuts financed by printing money. Obviously this requires coordination between the monetary and fiscal authorities, but this should be less of an issue in the US than it was in Japan.

---

[3]As Stephen Ross once said, to turn a parrot into a learned financial economist it needs to learn just one word: arbitrage. To my mind, economists are far too happy to rely on arbitrage assumptions to rule out solutions. Indeed, the second chapter of my first book, *Behavioural Finance*, is spent detailing failures of arbitrage (both causes and consequences thereof, including the ketchup markets!).

Finally, Bernanke argues that non-standard monetary policy should be deployed. Effectively, quantitative and qualitative easing. Bernanke has repeatedly mentioned the possibility of outright purchases of government bonds.

The Fed has followed this path once before — during World War II. As Sidney Homer and Richard Sylla write in their magnum opus *A History of Interest Rates* (gives you some idea what I did over Christmas!), 'Treasury war finance was based on a fixed schedule of yields. The Federal Reserve Banks bought whatever securities were required to maintain this schedule. Three-month Treasury bills were at 3/8%, one-year Certificates of Indebtedness were at 7/8%, short bonds were at 2%, longer bonds at 2¼% and 25- to 30-year bonds were at 2½%.'

Interestingly, Homer and Sylla note, 'When [World War II] ended, some people thought that the Treasury would not always be offering as much as 2½%. Perhaps rates as high as 2½% would vanish forever. Therefore in 1945, after the war ended, purchases of the last issue of 2½%s approached $20 billion. The Treasury indeed stopped issuing new bonds altogether.' This caused yields to drop to 1.93%! However, Homer and Sylla note that, 'This was the great crest of a 26-year bull bond market.'

One thing is clear. You don't want to be the last man holding bonds if the Fed goes down this route. This creates a beauty contest kind of game, where every bond investor is trying to second guess every other bond investor. Or as Warren Buffett put it (when comparing the stock market in 2000 with Cinderella at the ball, 'the giddy participants all plan to leave just seconds before midnight. There is a problem though: They are dancing in a room in which the clocks have no hands!'

Whichever combination of measures that Bernanke eventually opts to pursue his most telling comments come in the final lines of his speech to the Japanese policy-makers, 'Roosevelt's specific policy actions were, I think, less important than his willingness to be aggressive and to experiment — in short, to do whatever was necessary to get the country moving again.'

IS THE US JAPAN?

While deflation is all but guaranteed in the short term, I am not as convinced that the US will follow the Japanese route into a lost decade of deflation. As Keynes put it, 'The existing situation enters, in a sense disproportionately, into the formation of our long-term expectations; our usual practice being to take the existing situation and to project it into the future.'

My friend and erstwhile colleague, Peter Tasker (an expert of almost all things Japanese, having lived there since 1982) recently penned a note for my old shop on five key differences between the US and Japan.

First and most obviously, the US has had a much faster and clearer policy response than Japan ever enjoyed. For instance, the Bank of Japan (BoJ) didn't engage in any quantitative easing until 2001, some seven years after the Japanese economy first encountered deflation!

Secondly, Japan didn't really have any model to follow, the experience of the 1930s was a lifetime ago, and Japan's creeping deflation was a different beast from the rapid price-level declines that the US experienced in the 1930s.

Thirdly, Japan was hindered by fiscal hawks who constantly sought to cut back on fiscal expenditure. The fiscal expenditure that did occur was not financed by the BoJ printing money, nor did it have any real use (remember the railways to nowhere?). A policy of fiscal restraint seems unlikely from the new US president. When combined with Bernanke this could be a potent combination for avoiding lasting deflation.

Fourthly, there are pronounced social and demographic differences between the US and Japan. Japan's top-heavy ageing population made inflation a politically difficult solution. The US has considerably more favorable demographics which may help to make a return of inflation a more politically viable strategy than in Japan.

Tasker's fifth key difference is not so promising for the US (and is one that I mentioned earlier). When Japan was trapped in its deflationary spiral the rest of the world was doing pretty well on average. The US faces a far tougher external environment in which to attempt reflation.

CONCLUSIONS

As far as I can see there is no investment case for government bonds yielding around 2%. As Ben Graham said, 'An investment operation is one which, upon thorough analysis, promises safety of principal and a satisfactory return. Operations not meeting these requirements are speculative.' Or, as Keynes opined, 'The term speculation [refers to] the activity of forecasting the psychology of the market, and the term enterprise [to the] activity of forecasting the prospective yields of assets over their whole life.'

To my mind a 2% nominal yield is not a satisfactory return. The markets are priced as if the US is doomed to follow the Japanese example and enter a period of long, grinding deflation. While this may be the case, it is already reflected in prices, as such there is no value in government bonds. Even if yields were to collapse from 2% to 1%, investors would only make around 9% return.

If the alternative scenario comes to pass and the Fed successfully reintroduces inflation (leading to what Keynes so vividly described as the 'euthanasia of the rentier') then bonds look distinctly poor value, thus the risk is exceptionally high and skewed in one direction. As Jim Grant so elegantly put it, government bonds may well end up being 'return-free risk' (as opposed to their more normal nomenclature of risk-free return). If yields were to rise from 2% to 4.5% investors would stand to suffer a capital loss of nearly 20%.

Of course, there may be a speculative case for buying bonds. If the market is myopic (which it almost always is) then poor short-term economic data, and the arrival of outright deflation, could easily see yields dragged even lower. Thus riding the news flow may be a perfectly sensible but nonetheless 'speculative' approach. However, I am an investor not a speculator (as I have proved myself to be appalling at the latter), thus government bonds have no place in my portfolio.

References

CHAPTER 1

Dasgupta, A., Prat, A. and Verardo, M. (2006) The Price of Conformism. EFA 2006 Zurich Meetings.

CHAPTER 3

Baumeister, R.F. (2003) The psychology of irrationality: Why people make foolish, self-defeating choices. In Brocas, I. and Carrillo, J.D. (eds) The Psychology of Economic Decisions, Volume 1: Rationality and Well-Being. Oxford University Press.

De Langhe, B., Sweldens, S., Van Osselaer, S.M.J. and Tuk, M.A. (2008) The emotional information processing system is risk-averse: Ego-depletion and investment behavior. Available from www.ssrn.com

Shiv, B., Loewenstein, G., Bechara, A., Damasio, H. and Damasio, A. (2005) Investment Behavior and the negative side of emotion, Psychological Science, 16 (June), 435–439.

CHAPTER 4

Dinkelman, T., Levinsohn, J.A. and Majelantle, R.G. (2006) When knowledge is not enough: HIV/AIDS information and risky behavior in Botswana. NBER working paper.

Eisenberger, N.I. and Lieberman, M.D. (2004) Why rejection hurts: a common neural alarm system for physical and social pain, Trends in Cognitive Sciences, 8(7), 294–300.

Goyal, A. and Wahal, S. (2005) The selection and termination of investment management firms by plan sponsors, Journal of Finance, 63(4), 1805–1847.

Knutson, B. and Peterson, R. (2005) Neurally reconstructing expected utility, Games and Economic Behavior, 52, 305–315.

McClure, S.M., Laibson, D.I., Loewenstein, G. and Cohen, J.D. (2004) Separate neural systems value immediate and delayed monetary targets, Science, 306, 503–507.

Pronin, E., Wegner, D.M., McCarthy, K. and Rodriguez, S. (2006) Everyday magical powers: The role of apparent mental causation in the overestimation of personal influence, Journal of Personality and Social Psychology, 91(2), 218–231.

CHAPTER 5

Plassmann, H., O'Doherty, J., Shiv, B. and Rangel, A. (2008) Marketing actions can modulate neural representations of experienced pleasantness, The Proceedings of the National Academy of Sciences.

Shiv, B., Loewenstein, G., Bechara, A., Damasio, H. and Damasio, A. (2005) Investment Behavior and the negative side of emotion, Psychological Science, 16(June), 435–439.

Statman, M., Fisher, K.L. and Anginer, D. (2008) Affect in a behavioral asset pricing model. Available from www.ssrn.com

Waber, R.L., Shiv, B. and Ariely, D. (2008). Commercial Features of Placebo and Therapeutic Efficacy, Journal of the American Medical Association, 299(9), 1016–1017.

CHAPTER 6

Dijksterhuis, A., Bos, M.W., Nordgren, L.F. and van Baaren, R.B. (2006) On making the right choice: The deliberation without attention effect, Science, 311(5763), 1005–1007.

Green, L. and Mehr, D.R. (1997) What alters physicians' decisions to admit to the coronary care unit? Journal of Family Practice, 45(3), 209–210.

Reyna,V.F. and Lloyd, F. (2006) Physician decision making and cardiac risk: Effects of knowledge, risk perception, risk tolerance, and fuzzy processing, Journal of Experimental Psychology: Applied, 12, 179–195.

Tsai, C.I., Kalyman, J. and Hastie, R. (2008) Effects of amount of information on judgment accuracy and confidence, Organizational Behavior and Human Decision Processes, 107, 97–105.

CHAPTER 7

Evans, J.ST.B.T., Barston, J.L. and Pollard, P. (1983) On the conflict between logic and belief in syllogistic reasoning, Memory and Cognition, 11(3), 295–306.

Lewellen, J. (2009) Institutional investors and the limits of arbitrage. Unpublished paper.

CHAPTER 8

Einhorn, D. (2008) Private Profits and Socialized Risk, Speech at Grant's Spring Investment Conference.

Fama, E.F. and French, K.R. (2007) Migration, Financial Analysts Journal, 63(3), 48–58.

McCabe, D.P. and Castel, A.D. (2008) Seeing is believing: The effect of brain images on judgements of scientific reasoning, Cognition, 107, 343–352.

Minahan, J. (2009) Investment Belief Systems: A Consultant's Perspective. In Wagner, W.H. and Rieves, R.A. (eds) Investment Management. John Wiley & Sons, Inc.

Weisberg, D.S., Keil, F.C., Goodstein, J., Rawson, E. and Gray, J.R. (2008) The Seductive Allure of Neuroscience Explanations, Journal of Cognitive Neuroscience, 20(3), 470–477.

James Montier is a member of GMO's asset allocation team. Prior to that he was global strategist for Société Générale and Dresdner Kleinwort. He has been the top rated strategist in the annual extel survey for most of the last decade. He is also the author of three other books — *Behavioural Finance* (2000, Wiley), *Behavioural Investing* (2007, Wiley) and *The Little Book of Behavioral Investing* (Forthcoming, Wiley). James is a regular speaker at both academic and practitioner conferences, and is regarded as the leading authority on applying behavioral finance to investment. He is a visiting fellow at the University of Durham and a fellow of the Royal Society of Arts. He has been described as a maverick, an iconoclast, an enfant terrible by the press.